Learning *with* Nature

SAGE was founded in 1965 by Sara Miller McCune to support the dissemination of usable knowledge by publishing innovative and high-quality research and teaching content. Today, we publish more than 850 journals, including those of more than 300 learned societies, more than 800 new books per year, and a growing range of library products including archives, data, case studies, reports, and video. SAGE remains majority-owned by our founder, and after Sara's lifetime will become owned by a charitable trust that secures our continued independence.

Los Angeles | London | New Delhi | Singapore | Washington DC

Learning *with* Nature

Embedding Outdoor Practice

Los Angeles | London | New Delhi
Singapore | Washington DC

Claire **Warden**

Los Angeles | London | New Delhi
Singapore | Washington DC

SAGE Publications Ltd
1 Oliver's Yard
55 City Road
London EC1Y 1SP

SAGE Publications Inc.
2455 Teller Road
Thousand Oaks, California 91320

SAGE Publications India Pvt Ltd
B 1/I 1 Mohan Cooperative Industrial Area
Mathura Road
New Delhi 110 044

SAGE Publications Asia-Pacific Pte Ltd
3 Church Street
#10-04 Samsung Hub
Singapore 049483

Commissioning editor: Amy Jarrold
Assistant editor: George Knowles
Associate editor: Miriam Davey
Production editor: Nicola Marshall
Copyeditor: Sarah Bury
Proofreader: Audrey Scriven/Roza El-Eini
Indexer: Gary Kirby
Marketing manager: Dilhara Attygalle
Cover design: Wendy Scott
Typeset by: C&M Digitals (P) Ltd, Chennai, India
Printed in Great Britain by Ashford Colour Press Ltd.

Library of Congress Control Number: 2013955888

British Library Cataloguing in Publication data

A catalogue record for this book is available from
the British Library

ISBN 978-1-4462-8746-0 (pbk)
ISBN 978-1-4462-8745-3

For my family and friends, who surround me with love and support

Table of Contents

About the Author

 Claire Warden is one of the world's leading consultants and writers on the use of consultative methods in education. She works internationally to inspire and motivate people to develop and believe in their own practice, and that forms the foundation of her approach to self-evaluation. The centre of excellence she has set up in the UK is renowned for its Nature Kindergarten and the consultative Floorbooks™ used there. Her own learning pathway as a teacher included working in a wide variety of settings (2–18 years), mentoring and advisory work, lecturing at Strathclyde University, authoring more than 11 books and designing resources and landscapes. Claire founded the charitable company Living Classrooms Ltd to work with marginalised groups and within settings to develop the capacity of communities through connecting to nature.

Claire is an international committee member of the World Forum Foundation and is one of a leadership group of consultants who make up its Nature Action Collaborative for Children. She is a Research Fellow at Federation University of Australia, and is currently engaged in her PhD exploring Nature Pedagogy.

She works around the world with universities and colleges, governments and educators as an advocate for the rights of all children to high-quality, engaging education, inside buildings, outside in outdoor play spaces and beyond the fence in wild spaces.

Ways to contact Claire:

E: claire@claire-warden.com

T: +44 (0) 1764 650 030

W: www.claire-warden.com

http://claire-warden.blogspot.co.uk/

www.facebook.com/claire.warden.773

http://uk.linkedin.com/in/clairewarden

Acknowledgements

My grateful thanks are due to all family, friends and colleagues around the world, who share my enthusiasm for educational innovation and continual improvement.

I would like to thank the following individuals (and their teams!) who have been with me on the journey to explore the potential of Diagrams of Practice (DOP) which are shared in this book: Lisa Cripps (Tasmanian Aboriginal Children's Centre), Professor Sue Hooglam (Acorn), Danielle Ramsay (Auchlone), Gillian McAuliffe (Bold Park), Lynn McNair (Cowgate), Chris Campion (independent consultant), Anders Farstad (Hval Gård), Andrea Welz (Sault College), Enid Elliott (Sooke), Regi Pippin (Spirit of Play) and Michelle Lawton (Stretch the Imagination).

I would in addition like to thank the team at Mindstretchers, past and present, with special thanks to Carol Towers, Sabine Mackenzie and Stephanie Pryor.

Thank you also to Professor Jack Whitehead, Dr Joan Walton and Professor Bart McGettrick of my doctoral support team for their inspiration and support.

Introduction

Outdoor learning is on a massive continuum of quality and form. In order to evaluate the nuances of what is happening, we can start by looking at the management of outdoor learning. We can take each key aspect of management in turn and consider its influence on our practice. The features that we have chosen to explore are landscape, use of space, resources, time and the adult role. The weather sits on top of these elements as unique and uncontrollable. The child is the wondrous element that moves across all the aspects, making connections in learning.

The aspects are on continuums from high structure to low structure. By considering where our practice sits, we can raise awareness in the whole team and then use development planning to take action.

The first aspect is the topography of the land and the landscape that we create or use on it. At one extreme, we could place types of outdoor practice that are bound by artificial equipment, surfaces and designs; at the other extreme, we could find settings in natural wild spaces such as forest and beaches.

The second aspect is space. The three spaces are inside, outside and the wilder spaces beyond the boundary fence. These are used in different ways: in the way we work in them, but also in the way we make links between them, or physically subdivide them for learning spaces.

The third aspect is resources. At one end of the continuum, the resources are highly structured and closed; at the other end, we have open-ended materials.

The fourth aspect is time, with subdivided and highly structured time at one end, and free-flowing, self-fulfilling play at the other.

The fifth aspect is the adult role, which varies from didactic over-structuring to the calm supportive structure of an almost silent presence.

All practice sits somewhere on these continuums. It is the interplay of all of these lines of continuum that creates practices that seek to define themselves in slightly different ways. Practitioners around the world are being asked to attach themselves to set outdoor models as a form of identity. Names such as Forest School, Nature Kindergarten, Nature/Nurture Zones, Moorland School, Barnehage, Wald Kindergarten, Beach School, Forest Clubs, Woodland Days, pervade the internet forums.

This book seeks to go below simple naming to look at what I call 'Nature Pedagogy' – the understanding of *how we work with* nature in all of its forms. As professionals, we should attach ourselves to a set of pedagogical values that are created through thinking about our practice, rather than dividing up nature and dividing colleagues into separate silos.

In order to embed outdoor learning in our work, we first need to know what it is that we are doing. We need to deconstruct in order to reconstruct our understanding. This book challenges standard ways of approaching self-evaluation to offer a fresh approach with innovative ways of sharing ways of knowing and planning for improvement.

Diagrams of Practice (DOP) are a method of showing what you do in a diagrammatic form, using colour, line, size, form and pattern. They have been applied through research to explore how they enrich and motivate staff teams to engage the improvement of self and setting (Internal Report, MacQuarrie, 2012).

The origin of this book sits at a meeting point of three values by which I live. The first is the value of justice, which is often manifested in having an influence or voice. The voices of marginalised groups, of the young and old, are often lost as they are viewed as having no value or opinion. Diagrams of Practice give all people a voice.

The second is love. In this context, a love of nature, and possibly that it, too, suffers an injustice in that it has no voice. The large-scale commercialisation of childhood is over-whelming; media and global connectivity have a very loud voice that stretches around the world, breaking connections to nature in its path. When we go to wilder natural spaces, there is no internet signal but, ironically, the connections will be stronger.

The third value is hope. Humans are part of nature and we detach ourselves from it in an almost self-harming way. We are beginning to realise the long-term effects of disconnection. There are now more global education groups, such as the Children and Nature Network and the Nature Action Collaborative, that are creating a solid advocacy body.

The book is structured to use the Diagrams of Practice. These are presented throughout the book to inspire readers to experience an innovative way of communicating outdoor practices.

- Chapter 1 introduces the concept of multi-modal forms of self evaluation and then asks you to self-evaluate your practice through the creation of a diagram. Each of the aspects listed above is explored and applied to encourage the reader to dig deeply into what is actually happening in the management of outdoor learning.
- Chapter 2 outlines research that surrounds the characteristics that shape outdoor learning so that we can root our practice.
- Chapter 3 explores the specific way in which we can look at learning with nature in comparison to learning in or about it. Examples of individual changes and strategic planning are incorporated.
- Chapter 4 explores the influences on parents and carers and suggests ways in which we can share our values and journeys strategically.
- Chapter 5 addresses outdoor observation, consultative planning and types of assessment.
- Chapter 6 shares the wisdom of practice (Shulman, 1986) through a wide range of settings from around the world which have used Diagrams of Practice to share values and pedagogical thinking.

1
Self-Evaluation of Practice

> **Overview**
>
> This chapter will explore how relevant research techniques can support self-evaluation and centre improvement. The Diagrams of Practice (DOP) will be introduced as a form of mapping practice and to generate staff discussion in order to deepen awareness and understanding of how outdoor learning can be improved and embedded in our practice.

Research is key to knowing what you are really doing. However, the word itself is often linked to a form of research that is removed from day-to-day experience. The dichotomy here is between what we see as quantitative and qualitative approaches to research. When 'knowledge' was being explored in Victorian times, the arts and the sciences sat together. Over the years, quantitative research linked to science became more dominant; it provided data and statistics that could be easily extrapolated to provide norms. However, the reality is that education is far from being easy to quantify, as we work with individuals who have emotions, and with many ways of knowing. This book seeks to bring together some quantitative research and to explore ways in which we can conduct self-evaluation and action research to improve our practice through the qualitative method of Diagrams of Practice (DOP).

Reggio Emilia has given educators a wonderful opportunity to explore 'The Hundred Languages of Children'. It suggests that we have a hundred ways of knowing and thus a hundred ways of sharing that knowledge with others. It is ironic, then, that we do not apply the creative, arts-based methodology of knowing and understanding to the adults who work with children. As a person who sits with a creative approach to my own learning, I access quantitative readings and then process them into qualitative diagrams in my learning journals so that they link to my emotional, social and cultural frames. This process of application and processing has taken many forms, such as word montages, anecdotes, photographs, diagrams and paintings. It is this journey of increased awareness and understanding that widens the mind and has, therefore, influenced this book.

Time to reflect on practice

There is a potential to expand our perceptions of real situations by moving away from narrative and towards creative visual representations. There are examples of how this approach has worked in a wide range of settings in Chapter 6. We can evaluate practice by looking at the use of space, resources, time and the adult role, and then go on to explore the more subtle elements of practice, such as culture and spirituality, as the team raise their understanding.

*Journaling
outside*

*Working
together to
create joint
understanding*

The concept of using graphics to share thinking has been developed into a narrower definition of a Diagram of Practice. This is a diagram or form that creates a sense of disequilibrium
in both the person creating it and the receiver of the image. These are created to convey
meanings that are in some cases expanded through narrative. The process of creating them

encourages group and individual reflection and conversation. Diagrams of Practice are effective at communicating messages for parents, staff and the inspectorate.

Working together to create joint understanding

There are mapping strategies that plot the distribution of children and adults in space, or perhaps the physical layout of the outside area. These give adults a snapshot of practice. The Diagrams of Practice used in this book differ from this as they try to move beyond observation of the amount and location of resources, children and adults to express other dimensions. An example would be the learning pathways across boundaries, or the child's use of 'wild' spaces where nature is presented on its own terms and is not 'cleaned up'.

This approach to the reflection of how we can learn with nature is relevant in that much of the research sits in the affective, emotional realm, which is hard to define yet nevertheless real and significant. It is the 'empathetic resonance', as explored by Whitehead & McNiff (2006), that we are seeking to share in a Diagram of Practice, moving the sharing process from a data exchange to a more empathetic connection or participation, so that the reader has a deeper understanding of the situation being explored.

When the arts are used to research and reflect, Barone et al. (2011) suggest that symbols provide hints – they do not denote. However, something important happens – people begin to notice. What they notice can become, and often does become, a source of debate and deliberation (Barone et al., 2011: 2). It is this disequilibrium that changes practices. It represents a shift in thinking, looking through a new lens that will in turn widen the mind.

Caputo (1987: 6) suggested that all people were 'to keep a watchful eye for the ruptures and the breaks and irregularities in existence'. This watchfulness implies a willingness to return to the 'original difficulty of things' by peering beneath the surface of the familiar, the obvious and the orthodox in a re-scrutinising (re-searching) of the world. It is in adopting this interrogative disposition that we promote a level of dislocation, disturbance, disruptiveness, disequilibrium that renders it sufficiently – even highly – useful, and, therefore, in this unusual sense of the word, truthful.

The Diagrams of Practice can represent many aspects of learning with nature. As practitioners, we need to look for the irregularities in the work we do, to ponder and question what it is children are doing and how we can support them, and try to consider what this looks like when we do it effectively. We can all try to explore different ways of knowing and try new ways of sharing what we know, and where we are aiming to move towards. If we can use these diagrams to connect people around the world to improve practice when learning with nature, then they will have served their purpose.

Winston Churchill (1941, House of Commons speech, London) once said: 'At first we build our buildings and then the buildings build us.' In the western world we have set ourselves on a road to believe that education happens inside buildings and have set up a series of tools to propagate that belief. In order to shift a paradigm of thinking to learning with nature, we need to create a new range of tools, approaches that support learning with nature, so that we can create a new concept of 'buildings' for education. The process of creating the diagram opens up important conversations with staff. This book offers a way forward, although the issues surrounding learning with nature are complex.

If we are to self-evaluate our practice, then we need to pay attention. Can the skill of attending be something that can be coached and developed? To what extent is attention affected by intrinsic motivation? Is it possible that some team members will pay attention to visual forms of communication rather than narrative forms? Development planning, in any setting, should be constantly evolving as the journey of improvement continues. The diagrams lodge thinking at the point when they are made, and may act as a stick in the sand that can then be revisited in order to reflect on practice. The meta-cognitive process has value in itself and can be recorded in a second colour on the first diagram or represented in a new diagram completely. While working with the groups included in the case studies, it was the adjustment and fine-tuning of the diagrams that evoked a real sense of attention to detail, and that demonstrated how leadership in the settings encouraged noticing, attention and mindfulness as key values within a wide variety of settings.

Outdoor learning is a core area for learning for all aspects of the curriculum:

- Children who play regularly in natural environments show more advanced motor fitness, including coordination, balance and agility, and they are sick less often (Fjortoft & Sageie, 2000; Grahn et al., 1997).
- When children play in natural environments their play is more diverse, with imaginative and creative play that fosters language and collaborative skills (Fjortoft & Sageie, 2000; Moore & Wong, 1997; Taylor et al., 1998).
- Exposure to natural environments improves children's cognitive development by improving their awareness, reasoning and observational skills (Pyle, 2002).
- Spending time in nature has been shown to reduce stress and benefit the treatment of numerous health conditions (Kahn, 1999).
- Nature buffers the impact of life's stresses on children and helps them deal with adversity. The greater the amount of nature exposure, the greater the benefits (Wells & Evans, 2003).
- Children with Attention Deficit Disorder are positively affected by the calmness of natural playscapes (Taylor et al., 2001).
- An affinity to and love of nature, along with a positive environmental ethic, grows out of regular contact with and play in the natural world during early childhood (Chawla, 1998; Kals et al., 1999; Moore & Cosco, 2000; Sobel, 2004; Wilson, 1984).
- Early experiences with the natural world have been positively linked with the development of imagination and the sense of wonder (Cobb, 1977; Louv, 2005).
- Wonder is an important motivator for lifelong learning (Wilson, 1984).
- Children who play in nature have more positive feelings about each other (Moore, 1986).
- Natural environments stimulate social interaction between children (Bixler et al., 2002; Moore, 1986).

However, the way that outdoor learning 'looks' varies across the world. The challenges that many people face when trying to embed it in the setting include:

- awareness and understanding of what learning outside looks like;
- physical access to outdoor space;
- structure of learning in the outdoor space;
- inclusion of the outdoor area in planning and assessment;
- involvement of parents and carers;
- development planning.

The Diagrams of Practice can support all of the issues above in that they evaluate practice. When the team audits their practice and considers where they are on a continuum, they can begin to consider what they need to change in order to improve.

Diagrams of Practice (DOP)

Diagrams of Practice can focus on one aspect of practice in detail or many dimensions. To begin our awareness of the diagrams, let us start by exploring some single dimensions that affect children learning with nature. When we look at the management of outdoor learning we can focus on issues such as:

- physical access to natural spaces – in relation to distance from the building, movement to, from and within the space, subdivision of space, and the connection in learning across multiple spaces;

- resource allocation and use – use and movement; type and function; choice and ownership;
- time spent outside in nature – structure and duration; frequency and connectivity to learner;
- adult role and relationship – style of interaction; perception of role; methodology of teaching and learning.

Each of these sits along a continuum of structure, where many dynamics interplay to create the phenomena of experience that makes learning with nature effective. For the ease of communication and to encourage attention, the diagrams have been simplified to look at single dimensions. The integrated diagrams are presented in Chapter 6.

Space

Outdoor spaces for children vary between small hard-surfaced areas and large nature play areas with trees and grass. However, what we have in our space does not mean that we use it frequently, or that we make connections to it in our learning programmes. In the diagrams that follow, we look at three aspects of space: connection in learning between spaces; consideration of use of transitional spaces; and the use of spaces beyond the fenced outdoor area.

In many situations, the outdoor space is directly accessed through a patio door. However, the doorstep seems to create a perceptual boundary that affects what happens outside. Whole curriculum provision is put aside for an over-reliance on physical play; the space beyond the doorstep can be seen to be less important than the indoor space; and the intentional teaching of experiences and opportunities that link the inside (I) to the outside (O) and beyond (B) is not apparent. The diagram below shows the distance between circles as it indicates adult perception of the linkage between spaces (DOP 1:1).

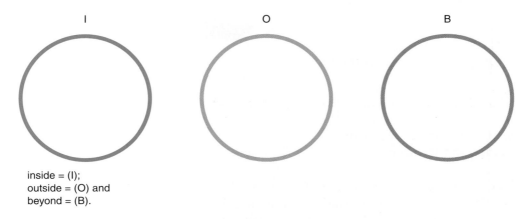

inside = (I);
outside = (O) and
beyond = (B).

DOP 1:1   *Connection in learning between spaces*

An example as shown in DOP 1:2 on the following page, would be the creation of transitional spaces that are used between physical spaces to aid the intellectual, emotional and physical transition of children and adults in meeting areas outside, cloakrooms, verandas, etc. (refer to the example from the practice at Auchlone Nature Kindergarten in Chapter 6, Case Study Two).

DOP 1:3 also on the following page shows the variety of options and forms that outdoor learning can take. We can work with nature on a beach, a moor, a mountain, in a forest, in urban spaces and in the desert. Nature presents itself in a variety of ways to people around the world. The journey is part of the learning experience and all the natural areas they visited are then used in an integrated way as multiple learning spaces, as shown by the black line.

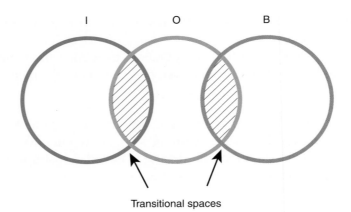

Transitional spaces

DOP 1:2 *Use of transitional spaces*

DOP 1:3 *Use of spaces beyond the fence*

These first-layer diagrams can be further explored through elements such as the following:

- Access routes and desired paths.
- Boundaries and territories.
- Transitions.
- Behaviours in space, journeys, meanderings, settling.
- The flow of learning between spaces (as defined by the intentionality of the adult).
- Multiple spaces which seem to support similar behaviours both in the centre/school and beyond into the community.
- New/infrequent spaces to raise excitement or intrigue.
- Frequent and known spaces that evoke traditions.
- Social justice – equality of opportunity.

Resources

Most of the issues surrounding resources link to the management of them. Consider where to put them, how to offer them and what kind of resources to use. The most effective systems are those that are reliant on a similar methodology to the indoor environment, and so are traditionally self-help. Open-mesh shelving with clear labelling, or carry systems such as a Tool wrap, allow the detailed support for learning to be readily available.

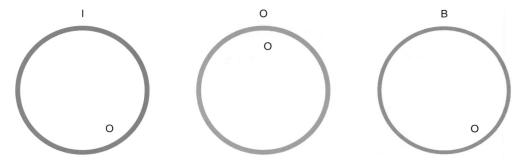

DOP 1:4 *Movement of resources*

This set of diagrams considers the movement of resources, the collection and movement of resources, and the type of resource.

In some cases, settings prefer to view inside and outside as separate spaces with their own unique materials and do not allow the transfer of materials across environments. In some bush school programmes, it is intentional that nothing is taken to the wilder space in order to encourage children to look at the play opportunities of the materials for the six-week half-day programme. This has been shown graphically in DOP 1:4.

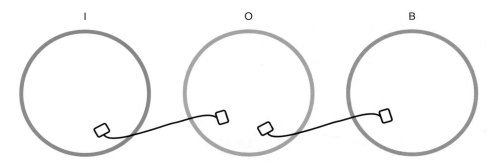

DOP 1:5 *Collection and movement of natural resources*

In this case (DOP 1:5), there is a key selection of the indoor resources that go outside and then some of the outdoor resources are taken to the forest. In temperate environments, this model can be seen in topic boxes such as fire people or in area boxes such as construction. The resources are put out in the morning, often by the adults. Weather fluctuations can affect the quality of the outdoor experience over the year if the staff rely on indoor resources that will be affected by the rain and snow.

The outdoor space works most effectively when it has materials in it that are designed to be outside. Natural loose materials such as stone, sand, rock, sticks and leaves can move across all physical spaces. Since they are full of play opportunities, they change in use (this is shown by the symbol of the resource in DOP 1:6). Nature's treasures can be brought back

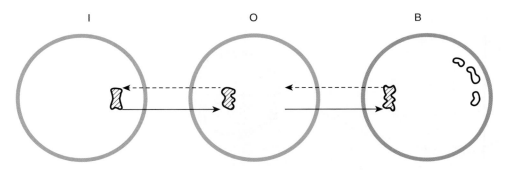

DOP 1:6 *The type of resource*

as transfer objects to aid recall and teach children about sustainability and harvesting in a practical way (this is shown by intentional planning by the adult in the solid line and the more open possibility in the dotted line). The spaces beyond can be the store cupboard for the connected experiences in the outdoor space.

These first-layer diagrams can be further explored through elements such as:

- access to natural materials;
- integration of embedded knowledge of the land;
- movement of natural materials;
- use of supplementary equipment;
- mapping types of learning and resources;
- levels and perceptions of risk.

Time

Children's learning is structured by time as soon as they enter a setting. We can, however, consider how segmented we have made time as a result of timetabling of learning.

In these diagrams, the size of circle was used to represent the amount of time spent in the space, not the size of the area. Segmented time is shown by the division of circles. The straightness of lines indicates the level of flexibility in timetabling that allows settings to respond and work with the weather.

This set of diagrams explores the effect of timetabled outdoor experiences, the linked use of the Forest School, and the connected learning experiences.

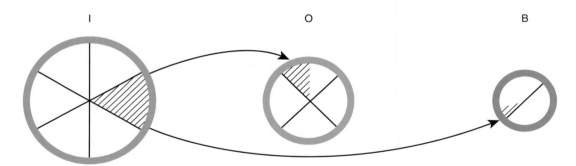

DOP 1:7 *Timetabled outdoor experiences*

In many settings, the day is timetabled either through visiting specialists, curriculum delivery or access to spaces. When the learning and teaching falls into a timetable, the effect can be to allocate outdoor play a 'slot'. Children need time to engage in learning, so sessions that are shorter than an hour often result in superficial engagement. Timetabling has an effect across inside, outside and even beyond if the adults have an activity-driven

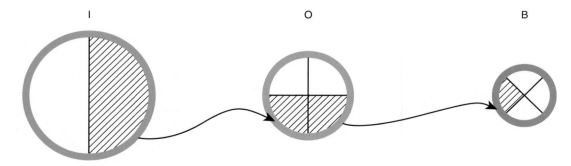

DOP 1:8 *Linked use of the Forest School*

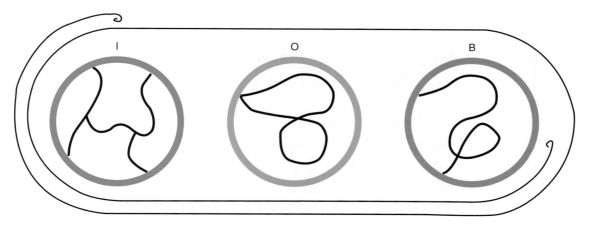

DOP 1:9 *Connected learning experiences*

approach. There is an increase in time flexibility across the multiple spaces, although this diagram (1:7) suggests taking a task from the maths curriculum, for example, to deliver in the outside area and a smaller task in the wilder space. The single arrow of direction suggests that there is little time spent processing or connecting the experiences after the timetabled block.

The next step on the continuum can be seen in DOP 1:8, as the timetabling inside has been simplified to allow the pacing to be shaped by the needs of children and the adult working with them. It can represent core skills and integrated learning in the primary school, or continuous provision in the early years. The outside area is still timetabled to have less time outside than in, but it has longer uninterrupted blocks of time when the children do go outside. Children go on a trip to sites, such as the Forest School, in the spaces 'beyond' for short blocks of duration and frequency (often six weeks for a half-day a week).

When all three spaces are given equal status, as in a Nature Kindergarten or a Green School, the diagram looks more connected, as shown in DOP 1:9, as the curriculum is experienced as spiralling across many learning spaces. Flexible timetabling inside still supports the teaching of core skills but in ways, and at times, that are authentic to children. The same approach to time is taken across all three spaces to give a consistent message to children.

These first-layer diagrams can be further explored through elements of practice such as:

- time spent outside;
- seasonal/weather-based variations;
- ownership of use of time;
- balance of time engaged in epistemic and structured play.

Adult role

Children need all the adults around them to understand why outdoor learning is essential for them. A practitioner's attitude, understanding and commitment will be key to the development of child-led experiences. Adults need to harness the special nature of the outside and be able to be responsive to the day-to-day changes nature offers. Reflexivity is an important aspect of the change process towards improvement. A low level of reflexivity would result in an individual shaped largely by their environment and the dominant group in the setting. A high level of social reflexivity would be defined by an individual shaping *their own* norms, tastes, politics, desires and so on. The practitioner needs to be the advocate for outdoor learning, irrespective of the team dynamic in the setting.

This set of diagrams explores adult views on learning, changing roles across outdoor spaces, and their approach to outdoor learning.

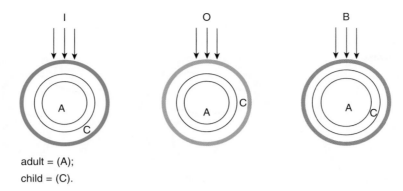

adult = (A);
child = (C).

DOP 1:10   *Adult views on learning*

When the practitioner views themselves as the director of learning rather than a facilitator, it will be a challenge to flex and change across increasingly more natural outdoor spaces. The way adults teach often follows the way they were taught as children. To support adults to change the way they teach outside with nature can take a long time, and DOP 1:10 shows little reflexivity. Top-down pressure, where the adult is in charge of children, is shown here with the experiences for children being directed by the adult. Spaces are viewed as separate, with closed tasks taking place with defined end results.

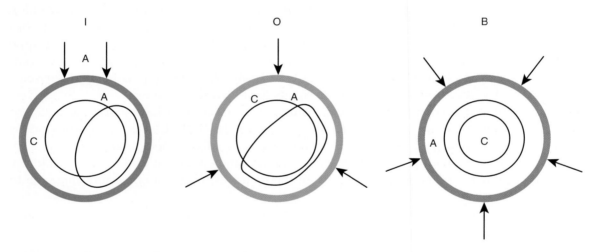

DOP 1:11   *Changing roles across outdoor spaces*

Another aspect to consider is the way adults perceive their role to change when they move outside. In DOP 1:11, the level of structure inside is balanced, and the child and adult interaction allows the child to have some time without direct adult input. When the situation moves outside, the adult role starts to move around the outside area as the adult takes on a security role. When adults perceive the hazards in wilder spaces to be greater, they increase the number of adults to increase the supervision, and revert to over-structuring children's learning to control the situation.

When the adult sees the children as confident and capable in nature, and see themselves as the co-constructor in the educational process across all environments, the diagram (DOP 1:12) begins to show some distance between the child and the adult icon. Children can be seen to have more freedom in this type of experience, where the adult planning is represented by decreasing amounts of scaffolding, as the experience moves from inside to outside and then into the wilder spaces.

These first-layer diagrams can be further explored through exploring elements such as:

- adult awareness of the significance of outdoor play;
- adult influence;
- adult reflexivity;

- adult interaction;
- approach to facilitation;
- importance of family and community;
- engagement of family and community;
- balance of adult roles, e.g. supervision of risk or support for learning.

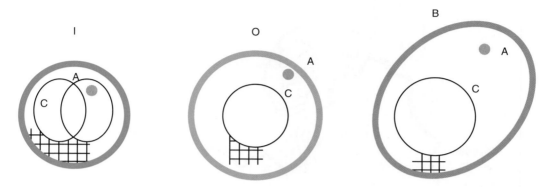

DOP 1:12   *Approach to outdoor learning*

Intangibles

Outdoor learning is a phenomenon. In order to self-evaluate our practice and then embed it, we need to consider many of the intangible aspects of being in nature.

The connection to land needs to be shared by the people on it and in ways that share their way of knowing. The longevity of these trails and paths carries a sense of tradition and shared understandings. DOP 1:13 was drawn on country in a sacred site in Australia, where burial mounds, clay pits and fishing grounds carry a strong connection to ancestors. The use of symbols allows diagrams to be drawn in dirt, on wood and on stone. We can consider this aspect when we create our own diagrams of practice. They don't need to be on paper; we can create them outside, and the graphics allow diverse linguistic groups to engage.

These first-layer diagrams can be further explored through elements such as:

- emotional connectivity;
- sense of gravitas;
- cultural connections and influences;
- spirituality;
- engagement and well-being;
- relationships;
- memory and meta-cognition.

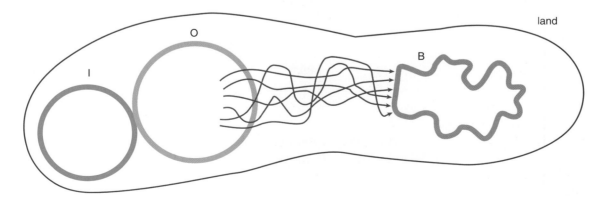

DOP 1:13   *Connection to the land*

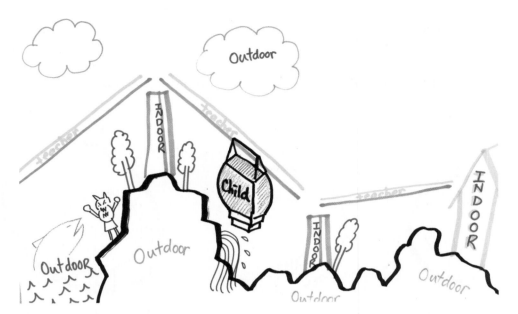

DOP 1:14 *Diagram of Practice (USA): Narrative and graphics are used to explore current thinking*

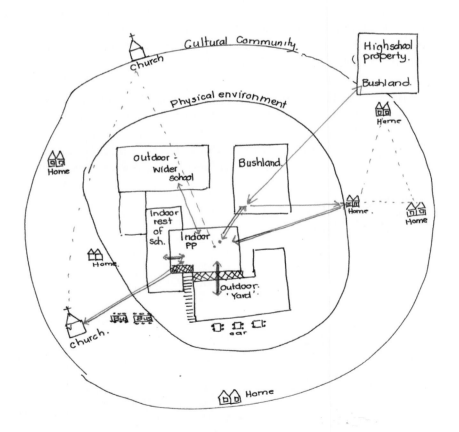

DOP 1:15 *Diagram of Practice (Australia): Creating a Diagram of Practice to raise awareness of place-based learning. Solid lines show intentional links – dotted lines are more casual*

As the initial diagram evolves, so does the thinking and reflection. This focuses the team on the detail and nuances of the outdoor experience. The narrative that supports the diagram warrants the inclusion of the learning journey of the adults, children and parents when they were creating it. Chapter 6 demonstrates the effectiveness of case studies and learning stories that were used to allow the staff to detail and discuss at the micro-system level, before moving above to see the larger picture or meta-system.

Let us now look at some Diagrams of Practice (DOP 1:14 and 1:15) by people from across the world. These have shown, through their first creative representations, the inter-relationship of children learning with nature. The adults and children come from a wide range of backgrounds, such as landscapers, engineers, environmentalists, educators, nurses and parents. Only a few can be shown here. The names and countries of origin have been left off to allow the freedom of anonymity, so we can analyse them.

Everyone has a different way to share their values and the embedded knowledge that they bring to that moment in time. They are influenced by culture and the wider society and yet hold onto the individuality of thought and emotion. Our experiences have shaped our practice, but we do not have to be slaves to the dogma of perpetuating a system that may not support learning with nature.

We can use these creative forms and also push ourselves to unravel the multilayered and highly complex set of interactions that make up the phenomena that seem to exist in any type of wilder space that children are in, whether this is a forest, beach, bush, creek, desert or mountain. The subdivision of nature disregards the concept of nature pedagogy in that it seeks to make a difference while the work shared here seeks to find the connecting threads.

The diagrams allow us to unpick the many layers of outdoor learning. When we create them we self-evaluate, we pay attention to realities in a style of auditing. This allows us to define a starting point, create an action plan and define where we aspire to be. This is development planning creative style!

Points for practice

- Use the core diagrams as a starting point. Put them on the meeting-room wall and try to build a composite diagram that shares the use of space, time, resources and the adult roles within your setting.
- Use overhead transparencies to allow multiple layering.
- A facilitator can use the concept of the Diagram of Practice to start to map out the elements to include the views of children, parents and staff.

Further reading

BARONE, T. & EISNER, E.W. 2011. *Arts Based Research*. Thousand Oaks, CA: Sage.

CAPUTO, J.D. 1987. *Radical Hermeneutics: Repetition, Deconstruction, and the Hermeneutic Project*. Bloomington, IN: University of Indiana Press.

WARDEN, C. 2010. *Nature Kindergartens*. Auchterarder, Scotland: Mindstretchers.

WHITEHEAD, J. & MCNIFF, J. 2006. *Action Research: Living Theory*. London: Sage.

2
Characteristics of Outdoor Learning

Overview

In Chapter 1, we explored time, space, resources and the adult role as possible nodes for a self-evaluation of practice in the management of outdoor learning. In Chapter 2, we will consider the characteristics of outdoor learning that are more intangible, but have a key part to play in the dynamic of the experience.

When we consider the almost intangible facets of outdoor learning, such as reflexivity of relationships, risk, social justice and inclusivity, ownership and empowerment, we can begin to consider their effect on the quality of outdoor learning.

Once we become aware of their influence on outdoor learning, we begin to notice. At the point when we are mindfully aware, we can then in turn begin to deepen our understanding through the self-evaluation process. Developing subtle changes in interactions and value-based thinking can take a very long time and does involve a process of self-reflection. To aid the process of reflection, this chapter will include some reflective questions that can be used for group reflection or reflexive thinking.

It is important to be mindful that our assumptions are based on a realised 'truth' that has been considered and presented through different forms of research. The origin of research will undoubtedly affect the presentation of the material. Over the last 25 years, I have explored my own thoughts on outdoor learning and have settled on the phrase 'nature pedagogy' (Warden, 2013a: x) as a phrase that encompasses my values and beliefs. The definition of a range of models of outdoor learning that are applied to working with children and families from birth to 11 years of age is covered elsewhere. Suffice it to say that, as a group of professionals, we need to engage in deeper philosophical debates around the underpinning values and beliefs before the creation of experiences and outcomes for children. If we understand the foundations of belief then we have a conceptual framework to consider and to evaluate the relevance and authencity of the experiences that we enable for children and their families. I would encourage practitioners to engage in a thoughtful journey so that their practice is personal, relevant and based on values and beliefs, not only for themselves as professional practitioners, but also for the community in which they work.

Let us start by considering:

- Should we be talking about outdoor play? Or outdoor learning? Natural play? Learning outdoors? Neither, some or all?
- Does there have to be a risk present for there to be effective outdoor practice?

- Do children 'need' to have an adult present for learning to take place? Is it possible that the relationship between the human and the environment is enough?
- Can we say that moving learning outside has a real impact or are we assuming that it does?
- What effect does ownership have on learning?
- What can theorists help us to be aware of in our practice?

As previously mentioned in Chapter 1, the purpose of this book is to encourage people to think, to evaluate their outdoor practice on a variety of levels and in creative ways. If we can vocalise our pedagogical views and be aware of how they have been influenced by our own experiences and supported by wider reading, we can be effective advocates for children in a diversity of forums.

Learning in, about and with nature

Outdoor learning/play/practice

The semantics of communication are fraught with detail, and yet the discussions and debates that arise from this challenge our thinking. For example, should the words be moved around to suggest learning outdoors as opposed to learning inside? In which case does the 'learning' really change across the two spaces, or is it the relationship between the learning and the environment that supports it that has changed? Is learning something that we can easily define as having taken place, or are we in fact observing involvement and engagement which may lead to a shift in thinking. If we assume that learning could be defined as the act of acquiring new, or modifying and reinforcing, existing knowledge, behaviours, skills, values or preferences and may involve synthesising different types of information, then it can happen without play in its purest form.

Play is used as a generic phrase, and (as detailed in Chapter 1) can be seen to exist in a variety of forms and spaces along a continuum of structure. The structure affects the interrelationship of the space itself, resources, adult role and the time allocated for the children to play with nature to create a fission, a phenomena that continues to be researched. In the early years educational paradigm, we are striving to reach a place of freedom and ownership for children within educational systems that have clear curriculum frameworks and structures for assessment and learning wrapped around them. Is it in fact an unachievable goal?

Practice is a more generic phrase that covers a wider realm of possibilities than can be detailed in play and learning. There may be times where an adult is modelling, guiding, listening, directing, overtly teaching within the outdoor environment. The range of pedagogical tools can all be present in outdoor learning practices. Does our 'practice' change when we work with babies in a nurture room through to standing on a mountain with a group of teenagers? If practice stems from our values, then perhaps it will not change in function but in form. As humans, we make subtle adjustments to our behaviours, both verbal and non-verbal, in response to the context of the moment.

Risk

Risk has the potential to achieve positive outcomes for children (Lewis, 2005; Nichols, 2000). However, there is an overemphasis on the place of risk in natural outdoor spaces. There are many moments when lying underneath a tree or watching a fly settle or a worm move cannot really be described as 'risk full'. Many people see risk as being an inherent part of outdoor learning (Beames, 2002).

Embracing the challenge develops emotional, physical and intellectual thinking

Louv (2005) brought the issue of risk aversion to the media through his work on the social situation that he termed 'nature deficit disorder'. The issue here is that, as a society, we have become hypersensitive to physical risk. Throughout my work, I have suggested that we need to be very clear about our terminology of risk and challenge in order to keep challenge in our lives but reduce hazards that are unseen and that are not within the conscious domain of the stakeholder. Challenges are chosen, hazards are not. Risk is the inclusive term that surrounds the total experience.

Let us consider that actually we should also consider intellectual risk and emotional risk as the other domains in order to be balanced in our thinking. How often do we do an intellectual benefit risk assessment on the possibility of boredom, or mismatched opportunities in a setting? Do we put an emotional risk assessment in place to change sarcasm and bullying in education? Intellectual and emotional harm can incur the need for long-term support beyond that of a grazed knee.

In our setting, which embraces nature inside, outside and beyond (Auchlone Nature Kindergarten in Scotland), adults can sense and observe children learning without falsely created limits. When children can *fully* engage with nature, the learning is full of higher-order thinking, problem-solving and challenge. Children appear to become strong stakeholders in their own development, as detailed in this reflection by the team:

> We have noted that over time there is an increase in confidence and competence, as children become independent and responsible for their own actions. They develop coping mechanisms, problem solving capabilities and transferable skills which also increase their self esteem and self belief. Children develop a respect for danger, hazards and experimentation. We can add to these potential outcomes by looking at the woodland environment – this natural environment is characterised by instability and this demands alertness by any user, regardless of their age. The children's Family Books (Chapter 5) give us a real insight into the children's views of themselves as adventurers and how the family feel about challenge in their children's lives. (Personal Reviews of Practice, August 2013)

Time to be in nature

There is a real need to include the voice of the stakeholder and to be able to value their involvement in the process. Many authors, such as Sandseter (2010), Gill (2007), Little et al.

(2011) and Buck (2011), explore the difference between adult perceptions of what is important to children and what the children feel themselves. When the values and desires of the family, child and setting come together, it makes the experience for the child so much more connected (see Chapter 4).

Offering children a risk-rich environment allows adults to help keep children safe by letting them learn to assess risks whilst guiding them through a progression of experiences. If risks are managed constructively during the play process, a 'child's desire to explore further' (O'Brien, 2009) can be fuelled. The best safety lies in learning through play on how to deal with it, rather than avoiding it. When discussing the possible risks of climbing trees, Jacob (4) stated that: 'only go as high as it doesn't scare you', while Francis (7) suggested that: 'If you can climb up a tree you need to be able to get down. Only go up as far as you feel safe.' Practitioners are demonstrating their belief that children have the right to choose to engage in challenge and test their developing skills.

The use of tools has become part of a wider woodland craft movement that is sweeping across some parts of the world. The presence of tools and a firepit in our outdoor areas are necessary, to keep warm or to be able to complete a project. Children in the Nature Kindergartens have access to a wide range of real tools – children aged 2 years have free access to tools such as junior hacksaws, hammers and so on and are able to choose the tools that they would like to use from a 'tree-wrap' suspended between the trees in the woods. Children also help to build fires and to light them with a fire steel. The fire steel is an intentional choice by the adults to help to ensure that children who have the manual dexterity to use the steel also have the maturity to understand the implications of lighting the fire. There are a number of policies and procedures in place to ensure that staff have knowledge of the safe use of tools and of lighting fires and that they support children to make correct decisions and behave in an appropriate manner.

Children are involved in the risk-assessment process

Children seek challenge and in the scandanavian countries they refer to that 'knot-in-the-stomach' feeling as 'is i maven' which translates directly as 'ice in the stomach'. This is seen as a positive emotion and one that both children and adults seek: 'Keep the exhilaration bordering on the feeling of pure fear; but if pure fear occurs, the play ends with withdrawal' (Sandsester, 2009).

The creation of a benefit–risk assessment is not simply a technical matter but needs to be a value-based exercise which is dependent on the practitioner's knowledge of children's capacities, their resilience and their ability to make judgements. There are static risk assessments of the site and the materials as well as a dynamic risk assessment that adjusts with the subtlety of behaviour such as children's moods and the weather. We use Ball et al.'s (2008) three questions as the basis of our dynamic risk assessments:

- What is wonderful about doing this?
- What do we need to be careful of?
- How will we stay safe?

Children enjoy being in wilder natural spaces. 'Wild', however, has many different presentations: from a toddler exploring a patch of grass to a larger whole outdoor area devoted to wild flowers with rolling hills and long wavy grass (Warden, 2012b). When we look at the three spaces of inside, outside and beyond, I characterise 'beyond' as the space that has the higher play affordance (Nicolson, 1977), a wilder space where we meet nature in an integral way, rather than being dominant over it. Through providing less structure resources and activities and instead giving more time to children to simply (or really complexly) 'be' in these spaces, is it possible that they can experience a psychological shift to connect to their wholeness or their subconscious genetic connection to being part of a larger system that gives their minds a sense of wildness?

Social justice and inclusivity

In the United Kingdom, we have a number of models for Early Education and, indeed, through primary school. In Scotland, we have many rural schools that have mixed age group teaching due to the small numbers in the setting. There are examples of practice where primary schools have strategically chosen to create groups of mixed age children as the benefits for learning have been shared through research such as Kutnik et al.'s (2007). At Auchlone Nature Kindergarten, we choose to have mixed age groups working from 2 to 5 years as it feels more like the family-based world with which children are familiar. It has a root in Frobelian thinking (Bruce, 2012).

Where there is mixed age working, the ratios for adults are set by legislation and must be adhered to. In Scotland, the ratio of adult to child is 1:4 for children of 2 years and 1:8 for children aged 3–5 years. It leaps at this point to 1:25–30 for children at the age of 4.5 to 5 years as they enter the more formalised school system. This can create a barrier to outdoor learning as the walls disappear and with them some of the practitioner's perceptions of security and control. Expanded experience and understanding of the deeper pedagogy takes time (AISWA, 2015). The schools in this project worked strategically to explore the perceived barriers of learning outside the classroom. The removal of walls, high child ownership and a changing of perception of the methods open to 'explore' rather than 'teach' knowledge, skills and attitudes were all explored over three years. At the point when we embrace a pedagogy that can move across the multiple spaces of inside, outside into spaces beyond the fence, there needs be a move from control to engagement in learning. The self-regulation and self-help skills develop a sense of social justice and inclusivity in the play and learning environment. Social justice is

*Creating 'relationship' and
social connection can be silent*

the child's ability to reach their potential within the social environment of the setting. When we move outside with children into nature it has an effect on them, just as they have an effect on it.

There are many common assumptions when we discuss the effect of gender on being outside. The assumptions that it is 'good for boys to blow off steam' or that 'girls prefer making petal perfume' need to be explored in training sessions so that the outdoor space sits without an implicit agenda. The greatest challenge may well lie in the openness of staff to explore themselves and how they are acting as a role model for the children. Do females saw and light fires? Do the male staff engage in transient art?

When we consider the management of children in nature pedagogy, we need to consider such detail as:

- modes of learning;
- individual rights/needs;
- children's understanding of and involvement in the creation of the area itself;
- procedures for using and moving resources (see Chapter 1);
- procedures for getting support and help inside, outside and beyond?;
- children's self-image as a person who 'is outdoors';
- movement systems to support inside and outside.

Individuality of exploration within a larger community of learning

Children bring their cultural realm with them as they come into the setting, this will undoubtedly affect their engagement with nature. The assumption of deep-level understanding and interaction through tokenistic experiences needs to be fully explored if all families are to have access to learning with nature. Cohen-Emerique (1999) puts forward seven aspects for when we consider the view others have of our ways of being outside:

- attitudes people have to their own and other peoples' bodies;
- understanding of space and time;
- family structure;
- rules of social interaction;
- ways in which requests for, or offers of, assistance can be made;
- religion or other belief systems;
- cultural change.

To be inclusive, the outdoor area has to be flexible and the staff should be responsive to the need for a range of solutions for outerwear, such as capes rather than trousers, wide-brimmed hats rather than knitted shaped ones and so on. The place of hand-washing and the use of gloves for some children is part of the daily routine, rather than being a barrier to learning with nature. Cultural competency is developed through relationships and deep-level understanding. Our charity, called Living Classrooms in Scotland, works with any marginalised groups, such as asylum seekers, former offenders, cultural groups in large cities, people new to Scotland and the elderly, and it aims to bridge the gap between nature and their understanding and engagement with it. Erikson (1998) speaks of the changing needs of humans as the move through their lives. Could it be possible that by understanding root human needs for nature and relationships that we could reimagine the location of homes for the elderly so that they can feel the cycle of living through their connections to the exuberance and energy of early childhood in spaces that embrace nature?

Reflexivity

At our International Nature Pedagogy Conference in 2007, the participants were invited to draw a Diagram of Practice to show graphically how they felt that the areas of inside, outside and beyond connected. The drawings could include key words that could share values and possible barriers. This led to the design of the Going Outside project, which was a two-year knowledge transfer project between the University of the Highlands and Islands and Mindstretchers Ltd. to research some of the barriers and challenges to outdoor learning (Internal Report, MacQuarrie, 2012).

In training sessions for outdoor play, the feedback has been collated from many countries for a period of more than 10 years. The evaluations indicate a wide range of barriers and support required before nature-based learning is fully embedded in practice. Statements, such as 'I needed ideas,' 'someone to re-inspire me to keep going', 'money for kit', 'getting it all done so we can go outside more', 'help with the fire and tools … they worry me', indicate issues of personal confidence and a deeper pedagogical belief of the role of nature in the educational paradigm. Larger studies carried out by Mannion et al. (2011) noted that practitioner concerns changed in relation to their perception of their level of expertise. The Diagrams of Practice in Chapter 3 explore this aspect of practice. As practitioners, we need to be aware of the subtle connections we have to children as they move between spaces. Our role at this point may be to have a conversation to connect two moments, to hold a memory for them to revisit at a later point, to remind them at that point of something that they have just done, an affirmation of dispositions or, indeed, a non-verbal eye-to-eye connection that says it all.

Use of tools to extend the experience

The conversation about qualifications is paramount in Scotland at the moment with the Workforce Review currently taking place. Scottish Educational policy is to develop a degree-led profession, with a Bachelors degree in Childhood Practice or a Post-Development Award (Level 9) being the recommended qualification for the head of setting. The majority of practitioners sit with a Scottish Vocational Qualification Level 3 in Early Years and Education or the Higher National Certificate (HNC) in Childcare and Education. The content of these courses has traditionally had a small reference to the role of nature-based practice.

There are a number of continuous professional courses, but they have become overly defined in some cases and too focused on ideas instead of on methods. The need to create identity in the professional world, however, is creating separate pedagogies and indeed professional silos. The presence of a qualification to go beyond into natural spaces, has in some cases created further barriers as practitioners feel that they cannot trust their own embedded knowledge to go outside into nature with children. The rural skills that programmes such as forest school support have in fact been in British culture from the 1930s, when organisations such as the Scouts and Woodland Elves were founded. The difference now is that they are seeking to integrate the experiences from social into educative time.

The skill set for someone to work in nature should be the same as those needed to work inside a building. Throughout the UK's history, we have adjusted our methods to be more relevant to working inside. There is a need to re-awaken these skills. However, at Auchlone Nature Kindergarten, the staff and children spend 80 per cent of the time outside and we have found that there is a greater need for emotional resilience required for the weather and a form of intuitiveness or reflexivity that the staff need. The child, natural environment and adult, all have an effect on one another to create a phenomena that is in its very nature hard to define. We need to be thinkers and researchers in these moments with children and yet be aware of the effect that we are having in that very same moment.

Ownership of learning to develop a sense of place

When we look at the plasticised, over-processed world that children live in, we can see how their learning has become secondhand. They receive imagery of trees and flowers without having actually laid underneath one and watch the leaves move or smell the fragrance of a rose after gentle rain has fallen. In the book *Nurture through Nature*, I was able to look at the world through the eyes of a 2-year-old. It was a luxury to have the period of a year to really listen to them and explore their fascination for nature through schema such as transporting leaves, enclosing pebbles or going through boundaries of tiny gates or stepping over lines of grass:

> Imagine a world where the lines were harsh and unyielding, the textures were consistent and variation is unheard of? Would it inspire you? Now imagine a place where the carpet changes every day, the ceiling is a myriad of different colours, light, shadow and movement. The feelings and movement completely surround you, sometimes breezy, sometimes cold, other times warm. Unexpected wonders fly by, sometimes full of colour and sometimes full of noise and movement. If we really want children to thrive, we need to let their connection to nature Nurture them. (Warden, 2007: 3)

When we explore the fascinations of childhood, we can begin to understand how a young child can spend hours in a sandpit with water flowing into it. Yet, even with this embedded wisdom, we still put children in strangely detached spaces that have limited authenticity to them. We create areas that have taken away the responsibility for discovery and personal drive from the child and replaced it with a form of learned helplessness that waits for structure from an adult. When children learn to receive knowledge, it adjusts their own sense of place as it affects their understanding of themselves within it.

Valuing authenticity in childhood

The Scottish Government's School Estate Strategy within the Building Better Schools in 2009 required local authorities to 'consider how to make the best use of school grounds and the outdoor spaces as an integral part of the learning environment ensuring that landscape design is at a par with building design'. The school grounds have taken shape and the curricular framework of the Curriculum for Excellence states very clearly that there should be learning inside that flows outside and vice versa.

In many settings, the outdoor area is very small for the number of children present. In order to extend the experiences for children, natural sites are found beyond the fence to which the children can travel. Repeated experiences on a familiar site was explored in the work of Gruenewald (2003a–b) as he developed a pedagogy of place. In his work, he explores the suggestion that, as humans, we create a relationship between ourselves and the experience of being in a place. This experience can only be 'true' to the person experiencing it. If we, as practitioners, can incorporate this by creating repeated visits to the same place, then this relationship can develop and deepen in a way that is more responsive and adaptable than structured tasks.

Experiential

One of the key phrases used within curricula is that children learn through experience. Yet, what form does this take? How do we know if the experience has had any response or has affected the child's thinking?

Kahn Jr et al. (2010) spent time experiencing nature in order to explore the way in which we develop a nature-language that gives us the chance to explore some of the deeper relationships between the mind and nature. How many human–nature interactions might there be?

Developing a love of nature

If we see the emotions such as joy, fear, happiness and curiosity as parts of the patterns, then there should be many different forms of experiences of being with nature that happen for children. The experiences of watching an emerging butterfly in a cage and within the natural world are different, but the question to ask ourselves is whether the emotion of awe will be the same?

Meetings and gatherings to negotiate situations

Kolb (1984) developed the term 'the natural cycle of learning'. He proposed that experience itself does not create knowledge but through reflection and analysis, learning may take place. His work has been challenged by a number of theorists as being overly simplistic, especially when applied to learning with nature. Argyris and Schön (1978) suggested that we need to apply the learning cycle to the self as we develop a new perspective. This has been expanded to consider a triple loop of experience to capture the process of understanding that could in fact only develop over time as experience provides us with a greater wisdom. If we take learning to be an internalised shift, the only individual who can truly be said to have learnt is the learner themselves. The learning moment where the new thinking is applied and tested to a new interaction may take place some time later, the nature world works in 'nature time' and our documentation needs to acknowledge that. It is, therefore, imperative that there is a place within the learning cycle for the child voice and the ability to revisit their own thinking to make the most of the experiential process (see Chapter 5).

The level of structure used in settings for the management of outdoor learning is explored throughout this book. In terms of its effect on the experience, Rogers and Freiberg (1994) highlight the importance of experiences that are freely chosen as opposed to those that are 'made to happen'. The importance of the emotional connection to nature-based experiences have been explored by Chawla (1998) and Waite (2007), and, in turn, the practitioner needs to understand that there needs to be 'trust' that learning is taking place in nature (Warden, 2010a: 31).

Cross-age working in family groups

Levels of involvement have been used to evaluate outdoor learning through a number of approaches such as the Leuvian scales, as well as Nakamura and Csikszentmihalyi's (2002, 2009) work on autotelic response, more widely known as the 'theory of flow'. It would appear that the closer the experience sits to learning *with* nature with all its capacities for engagement, combined with the desire and fascinations of the emotions in the child, the greater the chance that learning will be deeper.

Children and adults experience together

Points for practice

- Take phrases such as Outdoor Learning or Learning with Nature and then gather the opinion of staff as to their interpretation of the phrases.
- Take one of the characteristics that shape learning with nature such as Risk or a sense of place and create a diagram to apply the research to your own practice across the three learning spaces of inside, outside and beyond. What does the research mean for everyday practice?
- Changing beliefs and transforming practice requires sensitivity and time for such change to become akin to everyday forms of learning. Document the thinking around a diagram of practice at set points over the year to revisit and consider change in thinking, awareness or direct practice.

Further reading

Knight, S. 2011. *Risk and Adventure in Early Years Outdoor Play*. London: Sage.
Sobel, D. 2004. *Place-based Education Connecting Classrooms and Communities*. Great Barrington, MA: Orion Society.
White, J. 2011. *Outdoor Provision in the Early Years*. London: Sage.

3
Learning with Nature

Overview

This chapter will bring together the Diagrams of Practice and combine them with research to look at practical examples of strategic planning and management. It will introduce the pioneers of outdoor learning within their historical-political context. The dimensions of learning in, learning about, and learning with nature will be explored through the Diagrams of Practice.

There is substantial research and writing that supports the benefits of going outside and connecting with nature, as detailed in Chapter 1. The way we connect to nature (which, ironically, already includes us) varies in style. The Diagrams of Practice build up to explore the influencing factors that may be making a difference to the engagement of children with nature and the integration of it into a nature pedagogy, which is a method of teaching and learning with nature. The degree of structure in learning, and especially the nature of more self-initiated discoveries, have been explored in Pellegrini's (2010) research. He provides us with a continuum-based concept that allows adults to consider the longer journey of exploration of a methodology of working with children. There are many people who have supported the integration of nature into education. There are interesting connections through Comenius (1592–1670), Pestalozzi (1746–1827) and Froebel (1782–1852), which can then be seen to continue in the work of others, such as Seguin (1812–1880), who in turn, inspired a group who looked on education as an agent for social justice. Outdoor play and the incorporation of baths into early years settings were to overcome some of the living conditions at the time, where children could stay in one set of clothes for over a year. Fresh air was to improve health, good food was for growth, and love was to nourish emotional development. Owen (1771–1858) initiated schooling and improved health and hygiene for factory children in New Lanark, Scotland. A hundred years later, Montessori (1870–1952) was working in the slums of San Lorenzo, Italy, and McMillan (1860–1931) was doing similar work in London. McMillan started open-air schools, outdoor overnight camps and 'camp school' to offset the poverty and living conditions in the city slums. Steiner's (1861–1925) work focused on a higher spiritual aspect, which links to Isaacs (1885–1948). When she set up Malting House School in England in the 1920s, she demonstrated her view that 'children learn to exercise responsibility by having it' within a framework for 'unfettered' outdoor play (Isaacs, 1971: 102).

It is important that we place these pioneers within the historical-political context in which they were working. This gives us a greater understanding of why their approaches were rooted in education and health, although, ironically, many of us can see resonances with the health of children today around the world (see Chapter 4 for a more detailed look at Bronfenbrenner's work, for example).

The way that we work with nature across all approaches can be to teach about it, in it or with it. Many of the pioneers mentioned above worked with nature for health. This book shows that we can self-evaluate practice to increase the way we work with nature in our current climate of curriculum accountability. The effect of leadership and management of time, space, resources and adult role surrounding structure on each of these styles is explored throughout this book and is applied through the holistic nature of the case studies in Chapter 6.

Allin and Humberstone's (2010) research challenges the idea that simply moving materials or learning outside makes a difference to the way adults approach working with children in natural spaces. In order to make a difference, to make a persistent change, we have to have some kind of consciousness of what we are doing. The way we do this should vary to meet the learning styles of the adults and children involved in the process. Auditing may be a part of the process, but it should move beyond physical lists of resources to include an audit of practice. We can explore through Bruner's work on the spiralling curriculum (1960), and the links to prior learning that Vygotsky (1896–1934) examined in the concept of the zone of proximal development, and see how Wood and Wood (1996) extended this to include scaffolding.

So what are some of the subtleties of this changing way of 'being' outside that can be explored in order to support learning *with* nature? How do we create links for children across physical divisions of space? Practitioners in many countries have defined curricula and have a duty to explore the concepts, knowledge and skills within them, while supporting the learning capabilities. In order to simplify the process, these diagrams will look at the spaces and location of the outdoor experience and the learning pathways that adults are creating or, in some cases, of which they are unaware.

The diagrams explore structured tasks about nature and the effect of the expert on the practitioner role, and they use similar imagery in different contexts. Intentionality is represented by the dark blue solid lines (with direction noted), as there are occasions where the adult makes the start of the journey more defined than the review and reflective process. There are undoubtedly residual memories in the child as a result of experience, but these are often not discussed or extended by the adults. Thickness and density of lines are used to denote a strong link, and dashed lines represent a tenuous link in learning. The proximity of the shapes to each other is intentional as it attempts to convey the connection that children can make to them on a regular basis.

Learning *about* nature

Learning about nature is using nature as a thing to observe and learn about. It does not require any emotional connection or engagement from the child or adult.

DOP 3:1 explores what I see as being teaching *about* nature. In some settings, programmes of study teach about nature through very clear, structured tasks. The mini beast hunt for the biology topic starts in the inside space and then requires children to visit outside to gather materials or to observe nature in some way.

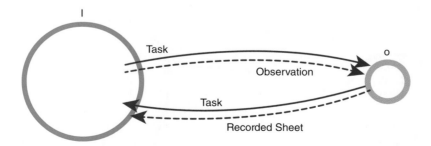

DOP 3:1 *Structured tasks to learn about nature (1)*

The effect of the expert on the practitioner's role

When children go on visits to field centres or places of specialist interest, such as a butterfly world, the practitioner's role starts to change. The transfer of the responsibility for the learning pathway can, in a simplistic way, move from the practitioner to the ranger or person in charge of the site, as the practitioner perceives that they have no specific subject knowledge and the balance of the power now sits with the 'expert'. Since the practitioner feels they have a reduced knowledge, the integration and connections for children with the setting are often short-lived (Bliss et al., 1996).

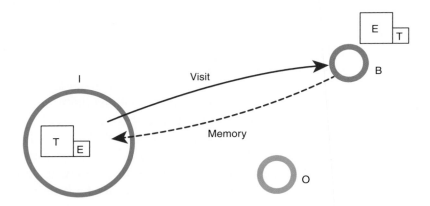

DOP 3:2 *Structured tasks to learn about nature (2)*

Some Forest School models operate in this way, with a centrally located Forest School leader who works in a park area. The children visit the site for short blocks of time every week for a set number of weeks. In DOP 3:2 we explored the issue of power balance in short term programmes. The expert (detailed here with E) becomes dominant to the practitioner (T). The visit is planned well in advance and can run to a programme that does not link to the experiences in the outdoor area of the setting or the curriculum inside.

Learning *in* nature

The second type of practice is the movement of the physical location of 'learning' from inside to outside.

DOP 3:3 explores the way practitioners learn 'in' nature without considering how the spaces can present learning in different ways. For example, in some early years environments, the indoor tables and chairs, resources and often décor are replicated outside, and in schools the lesson is unchanged in its delivery but taken to the outdoor classroom. There is no adaptation of the resources, use of space, structuring of time or change of methodology. In climates which have a wide seasonal variation, this type of approach has reduced children's access to outdoor learning (whether nature-based or not), as adult motivation has gone down as the cold, wet weather affects the management of resources.

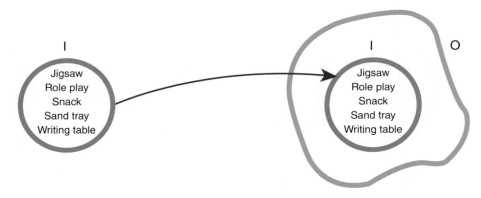

DOP 3:3 *Learning taken outside*

Learning *with* nature

The third style of working with children in natural spaces has become learning *with* nature. It sits as the title of this book as the examples from practice used throughout share how nature is embedded in the day-to-day learning of the settings. In many cases, a symbiotic relationship, which builds up a respect for the natural world, has evolved. It includes children and families as human entities within a bigger frame. Learning moves between and within the spaces. This practice is shown in DOP 3:4 as two way lines of exchange.

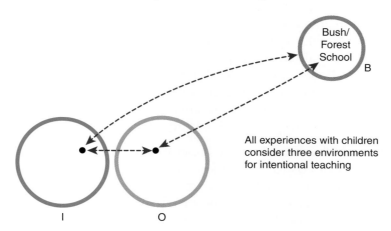

DOP 3:4   *Integrated experiences*

The key aspect that comes through the case studies is that the multiple environments have become embedded in each other and the strong links in learning are made visible for children, parents and community, and the adults who work in the space. Nature is integrated into all facets of the work. It gives emotional feedback loops to children about risk-taking, it supports and challenges the learning of core skills, and it bonds and connects children in social experience and extends the physicality of human growth.

   The nuances of time, space, resources and the adult give rise to many different models of outdoor learning. We could place highly structured, plasticised outdoor spaces with many boundaries and structures at one end of a continuum. The outdoor schools that exist in many parts of Europe and Scandinavia sit at the other end of the spectrum in terms of their practice. In the German centre (refer to DOP 3:5), parents drop children off at the edge of a forest at the start of the day, so the children can travel between shelters that are created by the community. Only resources in rucksacks are taken into the forest. The provision of large-scale toys and resources is kept to a minimum (Warden, 2010a).

   The use of research to underpin pedagogical thinking is important at every level in education. We can use the Diagrams of Practice to share thinking at a strategic level.

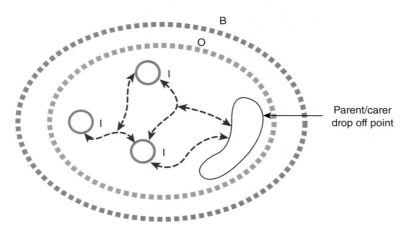

DOP 3:5   *Fluid learning across spaces*

Place-based education (Sobel, 2004) is the process of using the local community and environment as a starting point to teach concepts in language, arts, mathematics, social studies, science, and other subjects across the curriculum. By emphasising hands-on, real-world learning experiences, this approach to education increases academic achievement, helps students develop stronger ties to their community, enhances their appreciation for the natural world, and creates a heightened commitment to serving as active, contributing citizens. Community vitality and environmental quality are improved through the active engagement of local citizens, community organisations, and environmental resources in the life of the school.

DOP 3:6 shares a strategic overview of Bold Park Community School in Perth, Western Australia, which supports the core learning of children from 3–18 years and works as a focal point for children and families from birth. The whole school celebrates nature and supports the integration of the natural environment.

Sobel's (2004) *Place-Based Education*, along with Erikson's *Identity and the Life Cycle* (1959), work together to form the structure of an ever-widening journey from the 'nest' into the local communities and beyond, but always with a strong connection to home and community. The director of teaching and learning, Gillian McAuliffe, stated:

> In terms of pedagogy, I like to think of it as a dance. It is a dance which engages curriculum, students, teachers, indoor classrooms, outdoor classrooms and the 'wild' and built environments outside the school gate. This dance is characterised by the fluid nature of the choreography, with participants sometimes working together, sometimes separately, sometimes in small groups. The dance happens on the stage of life and engages those elements and the content which best supports the journey of the students and the stories they want to hear and tell. If this notion of a dance is understood, then the learning environments will be without walls and boundaries, and the integration you have identified is the natural and only way to go.

Having access to outdoor space would seem to be essential to learning with nature. In an ideal world, all children should have easy access to open air and natural spaces. In parts of the world, practitioners work in settings in war-torn environments, in areas of very high pollution, in areas where there is no space provision for outdoor play, or in areas of extreme heat or cold for long parts of the year where an indoor model can be developed that supports learning with nature.

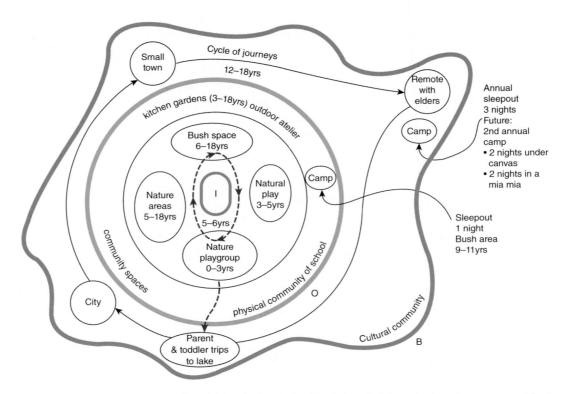

DOP 3:6 *Strategic overview of Bold Park Community School: Mapping out resources that link the elements of nature to 'between' spaces and into the indoor environment*

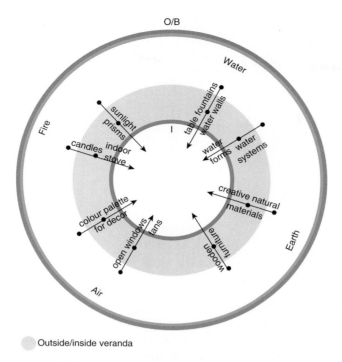

Outside/inside veranda

DOP 3:7 *Linking outside to inside through transitional spaces such as verandas*

Each of the natural elements exists in the outdoor spaces and the natural areas beyond the setting. We can create indoor experiences that take these elements and present it inside, so the only factor that is removed is the feeling of wind and sunlight, although in some spaces these have been substituted by using fans and daylight bulbs. Verandas can become an area that is half-way between, creating a transitional zone where nature has some protection. Through considering these nodes of learning (noted on DOP 3:7), we can intentionally put these into veranda spaces, and then connect them to another node inside the setting. An example would be a variety of live trees growing under the veranda, with log seating that connects to inside plants and smaller slices of wood for counting inside.

Extending the contact with nature by embedding it in the work we do gives children the greatest level of benefit, if we are intentional in its place and trust that it will support children to learn. In spaces where practitioners do not trust that nature can provide authentic experiences, we see a form of 'second-hand living', that is, the process of receiving information through technology, rather than fully engaging with it, to gather the essence of it. Is the teaching of the word 'tree', combined with an oversimplification of the image, even learning about nature?

Points for practice

- Is it possible to create a diagram that reflects nature pedagogy inside the home and setting?
- To what extent does the environment where you work resonate with one of the diagrams above?
- Intentional actions create strong links in learning. Take an example from your contact with nature and map whether you were learning about it, in it or with nature.

Further reading

ISAACS, S. 1971 edition. *The Nursery Years: The Mind of the Child from Birth to Six Years*. London: Routledge.
PELLEGRINI, A.D. 2010. Play and games mean different things in an educational context. *Nature*, 467, 27.
SOBEL, D. 2004. *Place-Based Education: Connecting Classrooms and Communities*. Great Barrington, MA: Orion Society.

4
Sharing Values with Parents

Overview

This chapter explores the way in which we develop a joint understanding of the value of outdoor learning with parents and carers. It will explore the influences that affect the parent and the family's connection to nature, and then explore practical ways in which we can work together to share thinking that can create collaborative improvement plans, effective documentation and increased family engagement.

In order to be advocates for children, we need to understand the influences on them. People believe that they have created their decisions about nature, rather than unpacking the subliminal influences that pervade all aspects of our lives in the digital era. Parents and families are under pressure from the media to move away from nature to technology, or to occupy all the moments in childhood under the guise of teaching core skills. Relationships with family are the closest, most intense, most durable and influential part of a young child's life, and yet many parents do not see the effect of global actions or political strategy until it actually affects their day-to-day life. Consistently present, enthusiastic adults help to foster positive dispositions

Engaging with digital technology

towards outdoor environments which may become enduring habits of mind and last for life (Muñoz, 2009). The transient nature of children's access to a variety of educators, or schools and centres, surely suggests that the emphasis should be on the central point of family and community. This provides the foundation to further enrich children's experiences to share the wondrous possibilities of nature through our education and social programmes.

Let us examine perceptions of education, especially nature-based education which suffers from being perceived as a lesser space (as being too affected by the weather, unstructured and messy). Indoors is seen as the key learning environment for the opposite reasons. We can gather from Beringer and Martin (2003) that we cannot assume that a change takes place when we go outside or that it is solely due to our contact with nature. Adults need to demonstrate conviction towards the value of nature in their lives, and not just in education. There are also confusions, both within the realm and purpose of 'education' and indeed from society as a whole, as to the way 'education' is presented, even down to our perceptions of the semantics of teaching and learning. In some languages, such as Russian, the word is the same. In the UK, our perceptions of what the two words represent are very different. The *Oxford English Dictionary* defines 'teaching' as the process of imparting knowledge to or instructing (someone) as to how to do something, whereas 'learning' is defined as the acquisition of knowledge or skills through study, experience or being taught. The subtlety of the concept, that teaching can include a collaborative experience so that the adult and child co-construct, is lost. Pedagogy, on the other hand, is defined as 'the method and practice of teaching', which allows itself to be more open to flexibility and variation. 'Nature Pedagogy' or the 'Pedagogy of Nature' is therefore the exploration of the natural methods and practice of working with nature that sit within a set of values (Warden, 2010a).

So what should parents believe? How should they gather information that is authentic? From the media? Or perhaps from the many parenting handbooks on the market? We need to be able to listen to the life stories and thoughts of the parents we work with, and then understand, define and vocalise, as a profession, what our values and methodologies are and why they work.

Sharing values

We will touch upon two theorists in connection to parents to help us understand the ways in which we can begin to share values. The first is a socio-cultural perspective linked to Vygotsky, and the second is Bronfenbrenner's bio-ecological model of environmental impact.

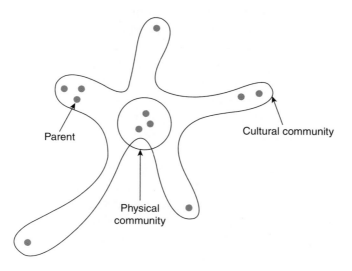

DOP 4:1   *Relationship between cultural and physical community*

Vygotskian thinking has influenced many of the structures that reside in social forms of learning, from the use of collaborative group working to the development of learning communities. Vygotsky (1962) argues that culture is the primary determining factor for knowledge construction. We learn through this cultural lens by interacting with others and following the rules, skills and abilities shaped by our culture. The Vygotskian approach suggests that children's learning is largely controlled by the environment around them. In order to develop both physical and intellectual capacity, the children need to develop 'tools of the mind' so that they become less subject to the environment and become 'masters of their own behaviour'. They become empowered to think freely. We need to consider the culture that envelopes not only the child directly, but also the wider culture of the school and centre and then the wider nuances of the community. Parents and carers will gravitate towards people who have similar values. When the value base of learning with nature is at the core, we can start to see how the community of a setting reaches beyond physical location. The style of a community school is based on the concept of value-based behaviour. This manifests itself in the integration of the parents and carers into the day-to-day experiences or management of the setting. The diagram (DOP 4:1) explores the relationship of the physical community of geographical location and the cultural community that develops from living by a set of values.

When the family find a setting to which they feel connected, they will travel a long distance to engage with the culture of that setting. In an ideal world, there should be a range of high-quality provision for parents and families with clearly defined approaches, such as Nature Kindergartens or Montessori settings. The reality is that scarcity reduces equality of opportunity for those parents who cannot find a setting that meets family and philosophical needs. DOP 4:1 maps out the reach and influence of a setting. The desire to connect to a cultural community is high for some parents, especially in the rural spaces where the setting can be the pivot for socialising.

Bronfenbrenner's research encourages us to look at a process, person, context and time model which illustrates how these factors affect the environment in which the child grows up (Bronfenbrenner & Morris, 1998). At the risk of oversimplification, we can consider the experiences of children learning with nature within this frame, and then the connection to the place of parents and community in DOP 4:2.

There are a number of levels of systems that we can consider when we analyse the setting:

- Microsystem (person-to-person, face-to-face, e.g. school, family, childcare and neighbourhood). The microsystems are perhaps the easiest to observe in practice. The positive eye contact and affirmation from a parent as children jump in a puddle, the family taking part in sustainability days, the two children playing together on a log, children inspiring their parents to go outside, playing out in the neighbourhood, etc.
- Mesosystem (links and connections between the microsystems). The mesosystem emerges as groups of families start to connect. Children benefit from the interchanges in their neighbourhoods and workplaces: the practitioner connecting to the parent, neighbours connecting to each other through community groups, nature groups, families arranging play dates in nature. Centres start to link to others with similar values to create a nature network.
- Exosystem (major institutions such as the legal services, social welfare, media, fiscal spending, research, education policy). If it is within the belief of the culture that nature is not an appropriate methodology for teaching and learning, it will trickle down to the micro level and affect the child directly. Current workplace attitudes to flexible working to allow long weekends to go into nature, or snow days for skiing, or indeed to support parents to have access to outside areas in the workplace, are still linked to the ways of working developed for industrial work practices and not the technological age in which we now live.

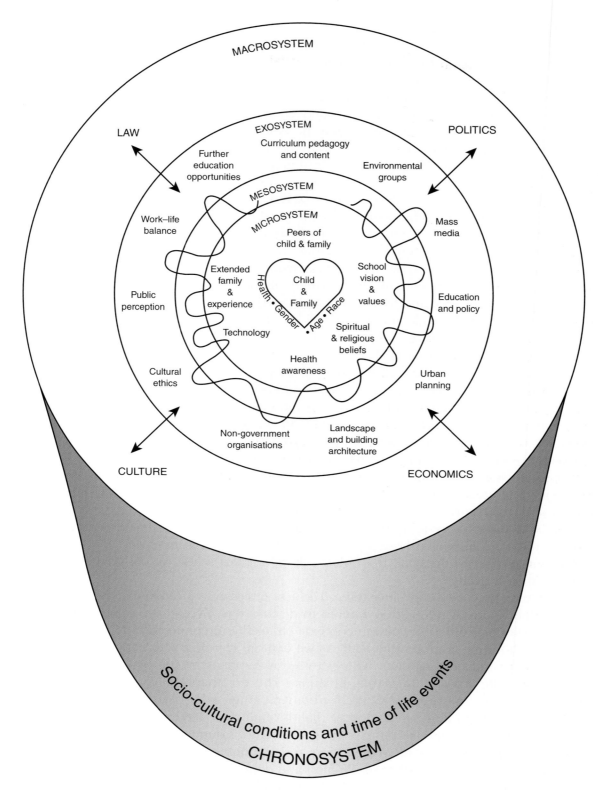

DOP 4:2   *The influences on the family and its connection to nature*

- Macrosystem (culture and other broader social contexts). Parents are part of the cultural system, and societal attitudes and values can be seen to influence many aspects, such as acceptance of risk, nature-based play, contact and access to technology. The Norwegian way of open-air living (*Friluftsliv*) influences a majority of parents' perceptions of nature-based play and risk-taking, whereas a focus on hygiene and protection certainly affects the way outdoor learning manifests itself in a large number of settings. Working with customs, laws and cultural values is key to widespread change for children and nature.

- Chronosystem (sitting underneath all aspects is time). This is certainly a feature that has an influence on children's and adults' connection to nature, whether it is time in the parent's own childhood to have developed the emotional memory that they can call on to help them develop emotional empathy with the desires of their children, or indeed current time during which they will allow their children to play in nature.

Bronfenbrenner and Morris (1998) suggest that time can be seen as constituting micro-time, which is occurring during the course of being outside or through interactions. It also constitutes meso-time, which is the extent to which activities and interactions occur consistently in the developing person's environment, for example, the frequency and duration of access to nature. It also involves macro-time, where developmental processes are likely to vary according to the specific historical events that are occurring as the developing individuals are at one age or another, for example, periods of war reduce the amount of time children can spend outside, or a time of recession reduces spending so that nature becomes a cheap alternative.

By considering these aspects in our practice, we can start to evaluate that practice in order to explore the lens through which a parent sees outdoor learning. Creating a diagram that considers some of these systems in relation to our own practice encourages us to reflect on how many systems affect both the setting and parents' attitudes and values. We can take from Bronfenbrenner's work that, as a profession, we need to move out of the microsystems in which we work, and gather people to engage with us from the other systems in order to consider the value of learning with nature. If we do not, the shift won't be large or consistent enough. DOP 4:2 attempts to summarise the influencing factors around the family connections to nature and therefore ultimately the child's access to outdoor play in the home and setting (refer to this, after Bronfenbrenner & Morris, 1998).

If we take the microsystems and the movement in and across the mesosystems, we can explore the ways in which these aspects may be manifested in practice.

We cannot separate the child from their cultural context when we consider how we will facilitate their learning.

Questioning practice is a positive thing. The action research question that the practitioners at Auchlone Nature Kindergarten wanted to discuss was: 'Would the same natural materials placed in two different cultural contexts be used and connected to in different ways due to the differing cultural influence?' As we explore learning with nature, would it then follow that a child's engagement with seaweed in Scotland would be different from that of a child on the coast of Tasmania, Australia? The dominant cultural view of a country can be slow to see the value of nature for human beings, while many indigenous peoples hold a deep and binding connection to this through their Elders.

The Tasmanian Children's Centre is sited on sacred ground outside Hobart. The centre is rooted in aboriginal culture so the Elders and community are involved in its day-to-day experiences to connect children to the land and culture. Children travel from outside the community to attend the setting. The building has been designed to flow and connect in order to support family relationships. Its décor uses earth tones and many community groups work within the building. Each room has easy access to the outside area and the team actively uses nature pedagogy as an educational philosophy. They look to integrate this approach into their way of working with children inside the building, in the landscaped area and beyond into the bush.

The collection of bull kelp from the shore line involved parents going to the areas traditionally used to collect it. It then came into the setting where an adult facilitated the skill of bull kelp bowl-making. This traditional knowledge is held within members of the community, and

Bowl made from bull kelp as an integral part of the day-to-day culture of the setting

through connecting closely to the Elders, the setting retains its connection to the land and creates memories in nature for the children and staff.

On the other side of the world, the bull kelp picked up on the shore of northern Scotland became a giant whip. It was carried, curled, wrapped, waved and returned to where it was found. Spaces on its surface that had indentations were filled with stones and shells. It was laid in hands as if they were indeed a bowl. The fascination was very high, but what was lacking as a visitor to this new material, even within our own country, was the wisdom of experience – generations of experience.

There appears to be an intergenerational amnesia when we call for a memory of connecting to nature or 'playing outside' in many parts of the world. Many of the younger groups of practitioners have very few stories to share of nature-based play and what they have is generally derived from organised play clubs. As DOP 4:2 suggests, the wider aspects of politics and economics have filtered into a form of reality significantly shaped by the mass media, including digital and global connectivity, that in turn alter the family's perceptions and attitude to outdoor learning, that in turn influence peers so that group support for nature is reduced.

From working across many settings, there is a general shift in parents' awareness of the place of working with nature. The perceptions of risk-taking, physical, emotional and intellectual freedom, and exposure to dirt have become negative. This is due to a lack of engagement as a result of what Louv (2013) refers to as 'habitual inside living where sitting has become the new smoking in terms of damage to health', where the emphasis is placed inside rather than on nature outside.

Sharing perceptions of the hazards of learning with nature

The characteristics of outdoor learning, such as risk, create barriers in the minds of people, both staff and parents. In order to move forward to learn with nature there needs to be a range of ways to share perceptions of risk. Many people focus on the tangibility of physical risk, yet few talk of the emotional risk of not being able to push personal boundaries, or indeed the intellectual risk of monumentally boring, inappropriate curricula. Evaluating where the parental community of the setting is in terms of their values and beliefs is important when trying to embed outdoor learning in practice.

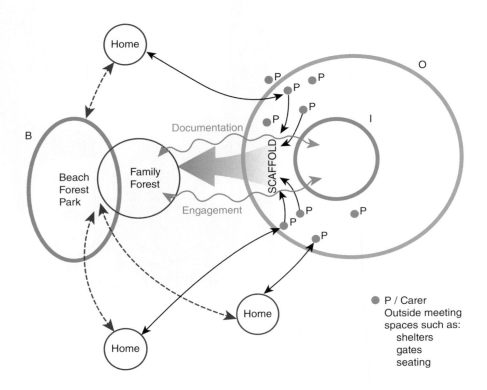

DOP 4:3 *Family Forest as a supportive approach*

Making the values of the setting visible and engaging for parents

DOP 4:3 seeks to represent the way in which a setting used a variety of experiences to support parents to explore the possibilities of being out in nature.

The parents have meeting spaces in the outside area, such as a turf shelter and kinder kitchen, stone and wooden benches and canopies, all of which support conversation. The documentation of children's learning is visible inside, in the outside area and within the 'Family Forest'. Parents are encouraged to develop the skill of 'noticing' and sharing their images and thoughts in the Family Books.

The setting takes those parents who wish to come to the Family Forest, where the staff scaffold some experiences such as den-building, petal perfume and cooking on the fire. In the warmer months, the parents sleep out overnight with their children in tents on the site with a member of staff. There are stronger links between the setting and some parents than others. As parental confidence in nature and awareness of the local environment and perceptions of risk start to change, groups start to meet as families in other wild areas, such as on the beach and in the park (shown as dashed lines in DOP 4:3). When this reflexivity develops in parents, they start to feel empowered and then they begin to connect with and gather together others who are like-minded, and so the movement starts.

Graphics and symbols are effective forms of communication as they cross over linguistic barriers. Using diagrams and graphics in a poster session can open up a greater dialogue than a policy document. Through displaying the posters, it can provoke conversations that can lead to the development of a community of practice (Wenger, 1999).

All parents need to be supported to reflect on their current perceptions, rather than practitioners expecting them to move to their point of view and understanding immediately. It is important to reflect on the starting point for parents in relation to DOP 4:3, in order to raise awareness of the variety of cultural, community and generational influences on families.

Sharing personal achievements

The national assessment resource of Education Scotland supported research into effective forms of sharing personal achievements between settings and families. The pedagogical journey of the community at Auchlone Nature Kindergarten in Scotland is in an electronic form to share (NAR, 2013). The reality of the self-evaluation and consultation was that it was done through a continuum book for improvement planning, a communication book with parents to gather opinions and the voices of the children in a Floorbook™.

The Family Books build on the concept of Learning Stories (Carr, 2001) to create a link between the people influencing children's experiences.

The Family Books (Warden, 2013c; NAR, 2013) are books collated over several years that incorporate the family outside the setting and the experiences within the three physical areas of inside, outside and beyond. These have provided the team with a real insight into the connection children have to nature outside the setting and the aspects that parents choose to share as being valuable. It is these long-term conversations that create long-term change in the values of the setting and the families who attend.

Sharing improvement plans

Self-evaluation is the first step in improvement. What we do as a setting, what people think of it and identifying the areas for development lead us to consider the forms of outdoor learning improvement plans. We have often put the arts-based thinking aside when we create our development plans and it may be that it is for this reason that many people dread the process. If we take the concept of the learning journey and apply it to adults, we can use a concertina-styled 'continuum book' (Warden, 2010b) to record the improvement/development plan alongside minimal regulatory forms. The third image on

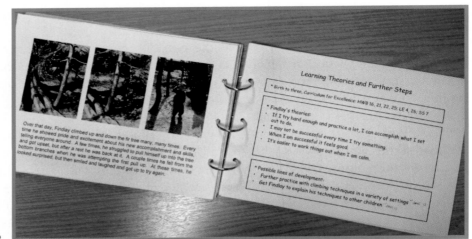

Family Books to share multiple perspectives, including the child's voice

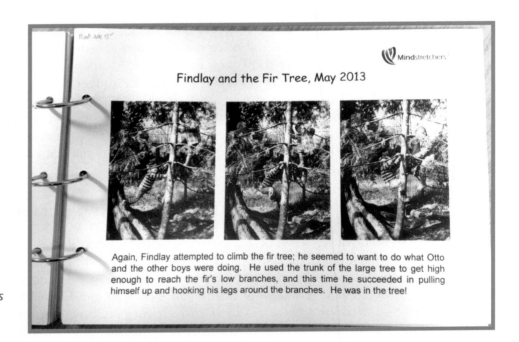

Learning stories that demonstrate the links in learning inside, outside and beyond

Creative and engaging centre improvement planning in the continuum book

p. 42 shows the development plan of Bolden School in England, which applied the concept to create a visual journey that inspires parents and staff to make the development plan a living document that they all enjoy. The actions within the continuum book should move across the systems from practical changes in setting, to community, to educational policy, to a wider cultural awareness in the media, so that the change process affects multiple systems.

The continuum book has a section for consultation and recording action for parents and carers, children and staff. The book is pinned to the wall or laid out for parents to clearly see the journey and the changes and improvements made.

The second example here is linked to the Standards and Quality Improvement Plan (SQIP) of Cowgate Pre-five Centre, Edinburgh, Scotland. Lyn Mcnair OBE states:

> There appears to be a move in the Inspectorate of Education towards the reduction of the quantity of paperwork for improvements planning … I do hope that this means we can explore other ways of communicating so that we focus on accessibility for children, their families and staff. A major focus for us this year was to develop our nature kindergarten. The following example is from the current research study (January 2013–February 2014) and our SQIP.

The focus here is a quality standard around curriculum, research and then the further development of the nature kindergarten. The rationale and design of the curriculum and the development of the curriculum, programming and transitions are all touched upon in the first stage of evaluation (this example is explored in more detail in Chapter 6, Case Study Three).

Pedagogical framing is based on our self-evaluation. This begins with a process of reflection, debate and reconstruction.

Field notes from observations at Stickland, the Forest School and the centre, and photographs and comments in children's profiles provided evidence of the persistent interests of individual children across three different settings, such as climbing and swinging on ropes, finding 'little beasties', or exploring slopes. The interview with J indicated ways in which children's experiences have brought new ideas and materials back to the centre and influenced the development of resources in their outdoor area. For example, the swing has been replaced by a hammock, loose branches have been added in parts of the outdoor area site and a water pump has been installed to give the sounds of moving water. Plans for a dry river bed are in progress.

Our practitioners show that with sensitive adult interaction, analysis and interpretation of play-based experiences can and do have a deep, well-conceived meaning to the individual child. This understanding relates closely to their holistic development. Our emphasis is on what children 'can do' independently and what they 'can do' with practitioners' support. Practitioners are guides who participate at times in play. Adults encourage children to offer suggestions and solve problems, for example, by using phrases such as: 'I wonder what would happen if…?' and 'How can we…?' These phrases invite the children to make the links between cause and effect, which generally encourages them to explain their thinking and extend their talk.

Real play belongs to children. At Cowgate, children choose the resources, the place and the children they play with. We view the curriculum as much more than 'outcomes'. The curriculum is geared towards adults waiting and really listening to children, and in so doing, those adults thoroughly understand what children can really achieve in all the spaces they visit.

What are we going to do next?

At Cowgate, we hope to extend the days when the children attend nature kindergarten. They currently attend two days per week, but the goal is to extend that to four days per week and further share our understandings with parents and other family members.

The content that has emerged through the creative thinking process is then transferred into the improvement plan itself:

Aim: further develop the Nature Kindergarten
Responsibility: links to Scottish national quality indicators.

DOP 4:4   *Development plan graphic to share principles into action*

The outcomes and impact on the children are then detailed as follows:

For Health and Wellbeing, some examples would include:

- Children will demonstrate high levels of stamina.
- Children will demonstrate high levels of resilience and will be able to sustain their focus for extended periods of time to complete their chosen activity.
- Children will explore, infer, predict and hypothesise in order to develop an increased understanding of the interdependence between, land, people, plants and animals.

- Children will be confident making marks and drawings using what they find in the environment.
- Children will recognise simple shapes and patterns in the natural environment.
- Children will show a growing appreciation and care for natural environments.
- Children will self-assess risks and be eager to challenge themselves.
- Children will be confident in using the outdoors and effectively take forward their own ideas.
- Children will be sensitive to, and relish, weather and seasonal changes.

The detail of actual change is then put into a written format to give targeted dates under the headings 'Tasks: By Whom?', 'Timescale', 'Resources', and 'Progress/Evaluation of Task'.

This form of written improvement plan will change practice, but it is not accessible to many people outside the senior managers of a setting. The team at Cowgate created a Diagram of Future Practice in order to increase the engagement and inclusion of parents, family and staff. The Diagrams of Practice are effective when working with parents and carers as they:

- stimulate conversation;
- build respectful relationships;
- make professional thinking more visible;
- engage all parents and carers irrespective of language and culture;
- use values and virtues as the foundation of practice rather than curriculum outcomes;
- use graphics rather than narrative to present practice.

Parents and carers can have a huge impact if they are aware of the choices they have and feel empowered to make them. Longer-term strategic change is effective when it is built on professional relationships that share common values. The Diagrams of Practice can enable all people to have access to and share in the process of embedding nature into the day-to-day experiences of children.

Points for practice

- Consider the relationship between the setting and parents in terms of the perceptions of the place and the value of nature. What experiences of nature and values do parents and carers hold?
- How close is the match between these values and the values of the centre?
- To what extent do the parents/carers connect outside the school community to go into nature?
- How does the setting facilitate family groups/events in nature?
- To what extent do parents and carers engage in documentation inside and outside?

Further reading

BRONFENBRENNER, I.U. & MORRIS, P.A. 1998. The ecology of developmental processes. In W. DAMON & R.M. LERNER (eds), *Handbook of Child Psychology*, Vol. 1: *Theoretical Models of Human Development* (5th edn, pp. 993–1023). New York: John Wiley & Sons.

VYGOTSKY, L.S. 1962. *Thought and Language*. Cambridge, MA: The MIT Press. (Original work published in 1934.)

WARDEN, C. 2010b. Creative Centre Improvement Plans – The use of graphics. Download article at: www.claire-warden.com/continuum books made by www.mindstretchers.co.uk

5
Observation, Planning and Assessment

Overview

This chapter explores the way in which we can support children learning with nature to make the learning cycle effective. It explores progression and continuity across multiple spaces through learning pathways and practical strategies such Floorbooks™ and Talking Tubs™. It provides strategies for children and adults to self-evaluate how effective learning practices are inside, outside and beyond.

Observation is part of building relationships. The human skill of paying attention and being aware of others' needs supports us to be together. Observations in education, however, are often overly complicated by the need to 'see' curriculum evidence. The act of learning something and the act of expressing that learning are different things but are frequently confused. If we take a simplistic view of learning to be the 'taking in' of ideas, then the representation of that learning is the manner in which the quality or quantity of the learning is evidenced (Moon, 1999). There are many models that seek to define learning and what constitutes relevant assessment procedures. All of these are bound up in the cultural influence of what is education and what is, in fact, subjective relevancy.

So much of what we do outside, and especially in the realm of nature-based work, is deemed to be purely process. It is the refusal to use the outdoors as an area to evidence the outcomes of learning that leads it to be deemed of lower importance when compared to learning that takes place inside a building. This does not mean that there is evidence that didactic tasks are of real benefit in the process of learning, but rather that we need to make the learning visible across multiple learning environments, so that they have an equivalence of status. It also does not mean that we need to use a predominance of summative assessment to measure outcomes rather than formative methods to share process. It does mean that the question still remains, that we need to look, as a profession, at the way in which we observe, plan and assess the outcomes of learning inside and outside.

The representations of learning can actually become another source of learning in itself (Eisner, 1982, 1991). The process of thinking of ways to represent thinking in all areas of education is at the core of this book. The learner who can repeat information is working at one level, and someone who is asked to explain it to another person will probably have had to internalise some of the meanings to be able to re-explain the nuances of communication. A graphical representation, such as a two-dimensional mind map or a diagram, will have the same level of learning as the latter form, but will be of a different type. The process of revisiting learning (meta-cognition) gives us another source of learning, that children can look at in documents such as Floorbooks™ (Warden, 2006), online blogs, narratives/stories made into books, film and photographic work, learning walls, documentation panels, both inside and outside, and learning journals.

When we are learning with nature, the time frame of the documentation needs to change so that children can *work* in nature time. If a child is exploring changes in nature, for example plants, it is beneficial for them to see the emergence, growth, uses, seed production, decay and re-emergence of perennial plants. In order to do this, the children need to be able to document their thinking over a year.

Making learning visible requires the adults to be creative and flexible in their understanding that the manifestations of the learning process will look different outside when compared to inside. As Chapter 1 suggests, we need to be aware that the adult role varies in terms of structure, that all aspects of learning should be experienced in nature in an holistic way. In order to observe children in this way, the adults need to consider some child development theories to help them create a framework that has a pedagogical basis. These theories support us to explore children's learning and development across multiple spaces, both inside and out. These approaches should be shared with parents to support greater conversation about their own child's interests, learning and development.

Laevers (1997) was interested in deep-level learning, which is about creating the right conditions in the place and the learner which can lead to deep-level involvement. This is combined with well-being. It is these two variables that tell us how children are doing.

Athey (1990) and Arnold and the Pen Green Team (2010) explore schema-based thinking. These are the repeatable patterns of action that children demonstrate when they are exploring the world. Common schemas are 'transporting', 'going through boundaries' and 'enveloping'.

Carr (2001) suggests that we observe the 'learning dispositions' rather than outcome achievement through Learning Stories, as the attitude to the learning process should be the focus of education.

Warden (2006) explores the frameworks of understanding, or children's theories, which are shared through consultative Floorbooks™ and Talking Tubs™.

Developing ways of seeing and interpreting what you see is often felt to be more challenging when in nature-based spaces as the 'normal' framing of learning is changed. When the framing is different, we need to train ourselves to look at learning through a new lens. Our definition of nature pedagogy is influenced by Whitehead and McNiff (2006), who view the learner as being a capable thinker, who has an embedded knowledge of their own living theories. The children have knowledge, skills and attitudinal opinion already within their thinking when they enter the setting.

Working on sensorial ways of opening up the knowledge of children from any age group allows the motivation of the contextual moment to be the frame for the delivery of any curriculum. The transformation of subject matter for teaching (Shulman, 1986) occurs as the teacher critically reflects on and interprets the subject matter; finds multiple ways to represent the information as analogies, metaphors, examples, problems, demonstrations and activities; adapts the material to students' abilities, gender, prior knowledge and preconceptions (those pre-instructional, informal or non-traditional ideas students bring to the learning setting); and, finally, tailors the material for those specific students to whom the information will be taught. Cochran et al. (1993) refer to this as 'pedagogical content knowledge'.

The pedagogy of nature is such that we need to look at the transformation of the subject matter. We need to consider the ways to represent thinking and to respond to the groups with whom we work. The challenge and benefit of natural spaces are the infinite variables they have (Nicholson, 1971). As 'pedagogues' in the space, we need to be able to work in a flexible way, as Shulman suggests. When working in countries that have different curricula, cultures and climates, it is possible to focus on a planning cycle that is framed around five questions:

- How can we be aware of what we already know?
- How can we learn here?
- How can we share our thinking?
- How can we assess our learning?
- How can we continue our learning journey?

Another question has to be noted here, as it is a point of challenge to many of us who work with nature. In many less formalised environments, we should consider the real intrinsic value of not over-processing the experience and pulling out the learning, and just trust that it is happening as a reflection of experience.

How can we just let the moment 'be'?

To develop continuity for children, we aim to support links in their learning from inside, to outside and beyond. These learning journeys ebb and flow across multiple spaces and can be supported or scaffolded by the adult, so that the threads are not lost by physical boundaries. The joyful moments in a forest can be remembered and given value within a classroom, while being extended and deepened to ensure progression through a framework of experiences and outcomes, to ensure breadth and balance of learning (refer to DOP 1:9, 1:12 and 3:4).

The relationship of all these aspects have led me to develop and work with Talking and Thinking Floorbooks™ and Talking Tubs™ (Warden, 2006), to create a process of consultative planning and assessment which places the child at the centre of the whole process, irrespective of age.

Consultative planning

Children have a right to have their voice heard. Strategies to consult them need to support the process of opening up the brain to the possibilities of a moment. With varying degrees of life experiences, the educator should support all children to contribute to the conversation. The Talking Tubs™ (Warden, 2006) are collections of three-dimensional (3D) and two-dimensional (2D) objects that are real and authentic, not simplified replicas. The intentional teaching takes place during the planning process for the contents for the tub, so that the practitioner is mindful of the possibilities. From observation, this 'pre-thinking' by the adult does several things:

- It raises awareness of the possibilities of learning with nature for staff and children.
- It develops interaction to be more discursive rather than question-based.
- It increases the time spent outside in natural spaces, as adults feel more relaxed about the learning process.
- It enables *consultative* planning within a framework of intentionality.
- The formative assessment, documentation and planning focus on the manifestations of learning and use engaging child-centred systems.
- It supports pedagogical conversations.
- The Floorbook™ increases communication between child, family and staff.

For children:

- It raises awareness of the possibilities of nature.
- It increases the feeling of empowerment and the affirmation of nature-based learning.
- It increases engagement and motivation to learn both inside and outside.
- It provokes thinking and raises engagement.
- It provides a way to share their own theories of the world.

The example given in Table 5.1 is linked to the outdoor experience of den- or cubby-building.

The process of den- or cubby-building is observed across the world, and is fascinating in terms of the cultural variations linked to many aspects of the activity. Examples include the internal framing of space or enclosure of territory, which are visible in the construction, such as the need for walls, fences and positioning, such as elevation on stilts, in a tree or underground.

We can use these aspects of biodiversity as a vehicle for learning through considering the curriculum, which is explored through using them. If we take the lines of enquiry that could come from a session on den-building, we can start to log the possibilities, and then extend the learning moment by offering provocations.

Den-building offers a very wide range of experiences that we can intentionally structure to bring out the learning, so that it can become our way of observing, planning and reviewing (the planning cycle). The children can differentiate through outcome, as the provocations are open-ended enough to allow them to engage at multiple levels.

In order to allow the children's voice to thread up through our planning, we need to define some boundaries, or the choices become too wide to manage in school-based environments.

The Talking Tub™ can be used:

- before or after den-building experiences to extend thinking;
- for dialogue/communication between adults and children;
- inside and outside (weather dependent);
- for 3D mind mapping (Warden, 2006);
- in small groups around a circular mat to support social interaction.

Table 5.1 *Talking Tub™ on den-building*

Line of enquiry (Main idea)	Objects 2D and 3D	Wondering questions (Q), Curriculum focus (CF), or capacities for learning
Location	Maps and compass; photos of dwellings on the ground, up a tree, on sand, on rock; photos of climatic and cultural variation of traditional forms.	Q. How do we know where to build a dwelling? Q. How do we create a shelter that suits the climate and landscape? CF: Mapping, climatic variation of building types, cultural diversity.
Territory	Door numbers, flags, totems, tradition of place.	Q. How do we develop a sense of place? CF: Identity, construction skills, cultural variations and similarities.
Properties of fabrics	Materials in a variety of absorbency (waterproofing, insulation); transparency (can lead to windows, patio doors, skylights), pattern, etc.	Q. What features of materials are important to consider? CF: Waterproofing, absorbency, opacity, measures and pattern, technology and design.
Décor	Photos of plant colour to discuss palette of shade and tone, furniture, mirror (e.g., reflection in puddles), wooden twig picture frame, lashed stick table, hooks made of branches. Diagram of floor plan to suggest rooms and divisions.	Q. What features do you feel are important in a dwelling? CF: Awareness of colour, reflections in nature, design and functionality.
Fastenings	Short lengths of a variety of ropes, straps, natural cordage with photos of plants that give us the materials.	Q. How can we make something to connect objects? CF: Technology, design.
Structures, shapes and pivots	Photos of types of den, such as bender den, Mia Mia, tipi, ridge pole, lean-to, treehouse, Geodome, underground den. Close-up photograph of lashing, knots, whipping, etc.	Q. How can we attach materials together? Q. How many different styles of shelter are there? Q. How did they all come to be different? CF: Cultural variation and similarity, structures and forces, tessellation and connections.
Nature of natural materials, e.g. wood, leaf	Species-specific behaviours, e.g. photos of Eucalypt self-pruning, Ash flexibility (hard wood/soft wood), leaf shape to repel water.	Q. How does the natural world cope with changes in humidity, levels of rain, temperature and sunlight? CF: Knowledge of the natural world, variation of species.

Documentation and assessment

The process of documentation of the manifestation of learning needs to reflect the ethos of the process. Thinking is at the heart of learning and as such it is for the adult to be mindful as to what to record and when to leave the 'moment be'.

The Floorbook™ (Warden, 2006)

- Is the working document that is a celebration of the group learning journey that can take place over long periods of time (from six weeks to a year or more).
- It holds many forms of assessment so that all types of learner can share their thinking and communication in a way that works for them and achieves inclusivity.
- It demonstrates links in learning from inside to outside and beyond.
- It makes the progression in thinking visible.
- It shares the child's voice, analysis of learning, next steps for learning, action and accountability to the frameworks of curricula.
- It is valued and kept to allow children to revisit thinking.

The first example here is from a group of children (7–11 years) who were working with our charity, Living Classrooms in Scotland, on a weekly Forest School programme. The Talking Tub™ was used after noting children's motivation to build and construct dens. The Talk around time took place inside, and some assessment of their initial ideas showed a limited knowledge of the possibilities for den-building. After the Talking Tub™, the group narrowed down to focus on structures, pivots and fastenings. The curriculum outcomes were put into the Floorbook™ by each group as they identified their own learning.

The Floorbook™ allowed the children to revisit their thinking from the previous week and to share that thinking across their working groups, so the learning was more integrated rather than being a 'bolt-on'. The summative assessment was done with a photo montage created by the whole group and reflective writing as individuals (see Photo Montage).

The second example is in the environment of the 2–5 years at Whistlebrae Nature Kindergarten in Scotland, the children had been in the forest at the base camp where there

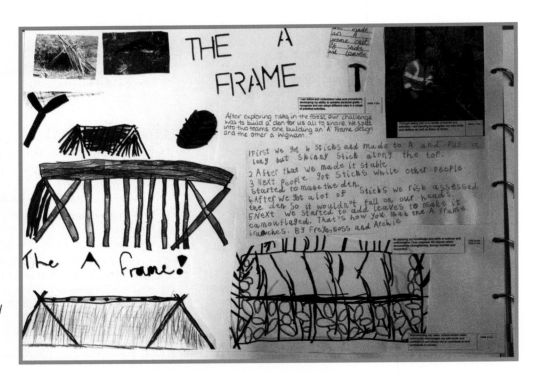

Graphics are used as a form of sharing understanding

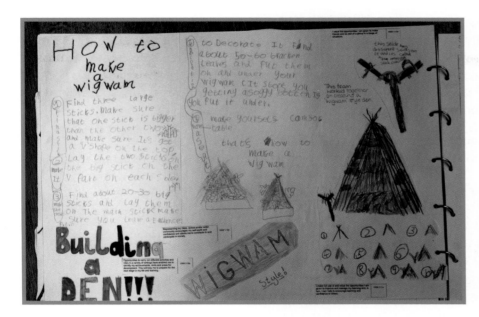

Sequence and detailed annotated diagrams are accepted as evidence of learning

Photo montage to share thinking by the group

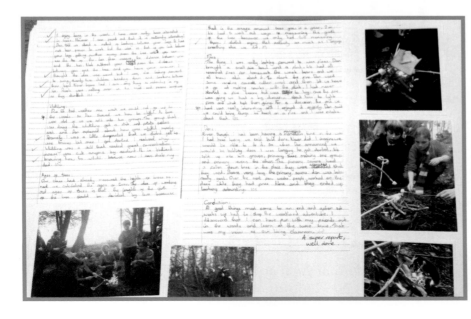

Variety of genres of writing in the Floorbook™

was a Geodesic dome for shelter. The cover needed to be washed, so the children decided to make a new one. Many learning pathways flowed across all three physical spaces. One main track has been shown below to demonstrate how to support children to make links in their learning.

The flow moved across boundaries and was tracked in the DOP 5:1. It started when the children noticed the need to change the canvas cover and then flowed through the following sequence over three weeks:

- The children designed the new cover (beyond).
- The design area had sticks, fastenings, etc. to explore the creation and connection of triangles (inside).
- The exploration of lashed stick triangles (outside).
- Talk around with Talking Tub™ on the essence of triangularity, tessellation and properties of materials as lines of enquiry (inside).
- The technology posts and ropes allowed exploration of the triangularity (outside area).
- Designs and ideas were drawn into the Floorbook™ (inside).
- Back to the forest to lash up the cover (beyond).
- Design of small geo-dome and 3D shapes (inside).
- Felling and transporting sycamore (invasive species) (beyond).
- Lashing and the creation of a small geo-dome designed by the children (outside).

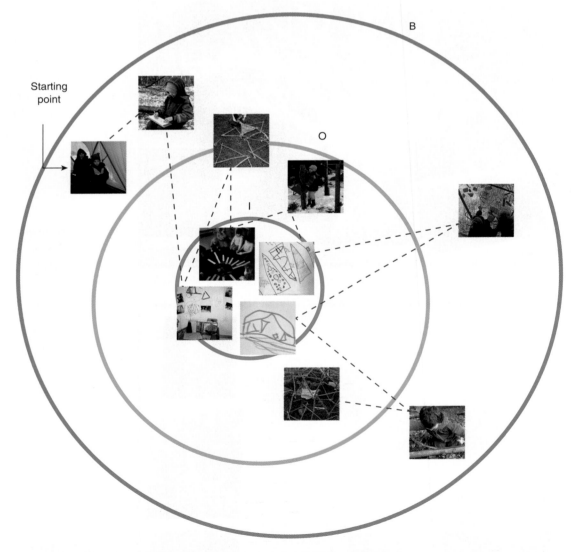

DOP 5:1 *Tracking learning pathways across physical boundaries*

Wrapped around these learning pathways were the intentional actions of the educators and parents. The idea of den-building still threads through this example, but moves along a Line of Enquiry around structures, shapes and pivots. The forward planning objective was to explore the essence of triangularity through the context of the geodesic dome; the children's voices through their plans and ideas, which were recorded in the Floorbook™ and the next steps noted and actioned with a date. Parents and the community wrote in the Floorbook™ to share in the learning process, and the detailed experiences and outcomes were noted and dated retrospectively at the back of the Floorbook™. Evidence was put into the Floorbook™ to show the progression in thinking about and understanding of the essence of shelter shapes, specifically, triangularity. Individual learning stories were taken from the Floorbook™ and put into the family books (see p. 42) and the Floorbook™ was taken into the book area to allow the children to continue to add their thoughts after the key focus had moved on, and to revisit the learning journey that they had taken.

Planning for sustainability

The level of integration of inter-curricular aspects varies across curricula. If we take sustainability as a common thread, we can self-evaluate our practice to discover to what extent we are embedding this in our day-to-day living:

> Sustainable Development Education (SDE) should be integrated into learning and teaching and be used as a way of delivering the curriculum and key skills. It should not be treated as an additional activity that is undertaken 'if there is time'. ... Regular opportunities to learn outside the classroom – in the school grounds, the local community or further afield – should be built into any SDE policy. (LTS [Learning and Teaching Scotland] & Sustainable Development Education Liaison Group, 2008)

In each Talking Tub™, there should be a line of enquiry to expand on any designated inter-curricular themes, as shown in Table 5.2. This can, in itself, become a focus for planning

Table 5.2   *Individual recording*

Line of enquiry (Main idea)	Objects 2D and 3D	Wondering questions (Q), Curriculum focus (CF), or capacities for learning
Sustainability	Small 3D objects if possible across all areas.	Decision-making
	Images and diagrams of wind turbines, a windmill, solar panel, wave energy. Washing line versus electric drier.	Use of energy; variety/efficiency
	Alternative forms of transport to get to the den; feet, horse hoof, boat hull, sky.	Transport
	Images of recycling boxes, compost heap, human waste management. Broken plastic object.	Waste management and duration of decomposition
	Natural food for foraging, images of waste and rot.	Food supply and use
	Globe to inflate to look at global footprint of food to eat in the den. Imagery of pretend money such as stones, shells and leaves.	Trade and value

and move away from a simple den-building context. The inclusion of the provocations frames the conversation and stimulates talk that is then recorded (orally, visual or written) as evidence of the children's thinking at the start of an exploration, during or as a summative assessment at the end hopefully to show progression.

The Curriculum for Excellence in Scotland supports child-centred assessments that are carried out in a formative style with the children. GLOW is the education network that all settings can access to share work. It is the portal for parents to access the community of learning for the staff, child and wider groups, such as local government. The more mature the learner, the easier the process of self-assessment and documentation of thinking becomes.

Gathering observations and processing them into practical actions that improve practice are sometimes used as an excuse for learning with nature. There are many uses of technology that can work in a positive way, to share the manifestation of the learning processes. The technology can become a positive influence as it allows the whole community of parents, staff and children to share in the journey with a wider group of friends and extended family across the world.

Ways to record and share the outdoor learning process include:

- portable electronic microscopes to record outside;
- electronic notebook/tablet;
- photo montages;
- annotated photographs;
- mind mapping (2D and 3D);
- genres of writing, such as reflective, lists, diagrams, prose, cartoons;
- learning journal;
- pocket reflective journal;
- blogs;
- electronic presentations of photographs taken outside and then put into forms such as Powerpoints, Prezi, Frame art;
- model-making across three environments with natural materials;
- use of art in weaving;
- sculpture with stone, wood, etc.;
- creation of music;
- head cam/waterproof cameras;
- films and audio.

In order to use multiple views to evaluate attainment or practice, there needs to be a simple approach that can transfer across ages and stages of development. I first encountered the graphics commonly known as 'spider diagrams' through Covey (1989). He used a spider's web to measure the consistency and quality of practice across a variety of points. The more balanced the area within the outline, the more consistent practice is. If there are peaks and troughs, they show us where our strengths and areas for development lie. The grading is done by an individual as self-evaluation or in collaboration for peer review. It can be done several times to give multiple views, such as child, parent and family and staff. If the master is put onto overhead transparencies, then the composite web will show where the different opinions lie. Easen (1992) describes the lens of the practitioner as being public and gener-alised, while the parent has personal theories about the development of their particular child. But the child also has a theory of how they feel they are progressing, and they will also have opinions about how well the setting is doing, even if it is in relation to themselves rather than quality indicators or curriculum outcomes.

Senior managers and educators benefit from the creation of overview Diagrams of Practice, such as that for Bold Park Community School (see DOP 3:6). Spider diagrams can then be used to gather further details and opinions from the school community about a specific area of the practice. This may be the detail around sustainability across the whole school, comfort in the use of tools, the experience of curriculum, or parental perceptions of risk. In the

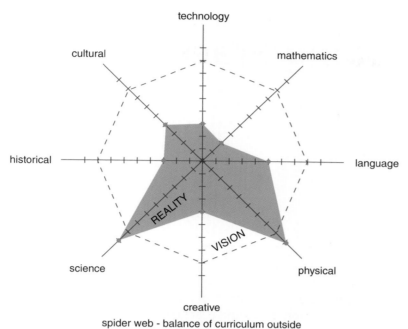

spider web - balance of curriculum outside

DOP 5:2 *Diagram to map assessment of personal engagement in curriculum opportunities outside*

example, we have taken a group of 9-year-old children and asked them to plot what they learn most about when they are in the outdoor classroom.

DOP 5:2 shows that the areas of science and physical play dominate. The diagrams can be dated and put into the personal learning journal or into the group Floorbook™ to show learning or the manifestation of it at a given point in time. This is a form of summative assessment as it marks a defined point. Through revisiting the diagram, children and adults can track achievement and changes in practice.

Children have the right to be heard and consulted about many aspects of life, but if the participation is not to be tokenistic, we need to include children at many levels in real ways (Hart, 1992). That includes the planning and self-assessment of their learning.

Points for practice

- Consider the level of consultation in your planning. How could you record the child's voice as the core of it?
- How could you raise awareness of the possibilities of outdoor learning for staff, children and parents?
- Is there a balance between observations made outside and inside?

Further reading

COCHRAN, K.F., DERUITER, J.A. & KING, R.A. 1993. Teacher pedagogical constructions: A recognition of pedagogical content knowledge. *Journal of Teacher Education*, 44(4), 263–271.

EISNER, E. 1991. Forms of understanding and the future of education. *Educational Researcher*, 22, 5–11.

SHULMAN, L.S. 1986. Those who understand: Knowledge growth in teaching. *Educational Researcher*, 15(2), 4–14.

6
Embedding Practice

Overview

This chapter explores the use of graphics and particularly the use of Diagrams of Practice to share elements of evaluation, changing practice and vision and values. A wide range of types of settings are included, from home-based care to large independent schools, and these cater for children, youth and families from birth to 18 years.

The process of developing an approach to self-evaluation, reflection and changing practice has to stand the test of experience and then sustainability. The settings in this chapter are working with me to explore motivational ways of engaging staff teams and pushing forward their conversations about how their thinking can be shared with others. Given that we know people learn and communicate in different ways, there needs to be a move away from purely narrative communication to consider graphics and art-based communication as well. My work has promoted and supported divergent thinking and creativity for over 25 years. This has been demonstrated through a range of evolving methods to record and reflect on the journey of improvement in the setting and with staff: a very large number of centres have explored Floorbooks™ and Talking Tubs™ at an adult level to provoke the possibilities for the setting and record the staff development journey; continuum books have been used by individuals and senior managers alongside more functional forms of recording to engage staff and parents; and now Diagrams of Practice have emerged as another tool to use to share the visions and values that we have and how they are working in practice.

These settings were given a framework in which to work, with self-evaluation prompts and suggestions for the creation of the diagram. Some worked directly with me, and others from a distance. The senior managers and the staff have created a range of graphics that share their thinking in ways that bring it alive for parents, families and staff.

CASE STUDY ONE

Name: Acorn Learning Centre, Trinity Lutheran College

Location: Everett, Seattle, WA, USA

Type of setting: Acorn Learning Centre has been developing over the past three years to become a model of an 'urban nature' setting in support of early learning for the surrounding community. It is the laboratory for the Early Childhood Education programme at Trinity Lutheran College, a small Christian liberal arts school. Currently, 12 children are enrolled in the Urban

Nature preschool, 7 in the afterschool programme, and 4 other toddlers who are children of the Trinity community. Acorn is located in Everett, a small city north of Seattle, Washington. It is surrounded by mortar and brick buildings, a grid of typical urban streets and large parking garages.

After studying at Mindstretchers with Claire Warden, and researching the many benefits of outdoor time, spaces and approaches to learning, an upper-level course was developed at the college called 'Children & Nature'. This course has been instrumental in changing the attitudes of students and faculty in this college. It has steered the course for emphasising nature in the Early Childhood Education Department (ECED) major.

Rooftop 'beach' area

The beginnings were modest. In 2010, two faculty members approached the administration with the idea of using the top level of the college's parking garage (car park) as a 'community garden and children's play space'. The possibilities for this becoming a community-building centre were enormous.

The problems quickly mounted. First, this was not a budgeted item, meaning that the college had no money to offer this dream. Grants were necessary to provide for materials and structures, and gave us the opportunity to construct a solar garden for capturing energy. Other monies became available to move our urban gardening ideas into the community. We now have eight community partners who grow vegetables from the start and that begin in the college's greenhouse.

Overhead view of rooftop garden, Trinity Lutheran College

With the limited funding, we realised that this effort was going to be a developing one and we continue to develop new areas, new ideas and new community partners annually.

In order to embed the relevance of the space, the garden provides vegetables for the college salad bar, as well as fresh greens for community food banks. It also produces solar energy equivalent to the electricity necessary to power a home and has a growing 'orchard' that will soon produce cherries, apples and pears for the community.

Most importantly, it provides a rich place for early learning. Grant money provided materials to build a 'beach' – a large sand area with landscape cloth tubes as the borders. Two meadows were constructed: a large one with a 'hill' (a very slight incline); and the other with a growing willow structure as a play area for the children. In addition, five small wading pools became a children's planting area. The staff observed the children flourishing in their outdoor spaces.

The Garden has many areas for student engagement. Besides the original 'beach', meadows and planting areas, Acorn has a Garden House to hold outdoor clothing, materials and equipment for gardening and for play. We have a new 'estuary' at the bottom of the painted 'Salmon River' that has become a favourite place for construction and sand play. We have a woodworking area and many large sections of trees for sawing, hammering and other creative endeavours. The creation of a rain garden, to process run-off water, added a large chalk board for the children's use, as well as a tunnel of running water during rain storms. Mason bees and a Monarch butterfly way-station were included. Strawberries, blueberries, cherry tomatoes and carrots are the favourite foods to eat. Children are free to pick and eat when the fruits and vegetables are ripe.

Factors surrounding the Diagram of Practice

Adult roles/staffing:

The Chair of the Early Childhood Education Department oversees the entire programme to support adult scaffolding rather than over-structuring learning:

- Lead teacher a graduate of Trinity's Early Childhood Education (ECE) programme.
- A student business degree major who handles all the scheduling and money matters.

- Skill level/understanding enhanced in staff as all have been through or are connected to the Children and Nature college course.

Time:

- Seasonal variations affect duration of access mainly due to length of daylight in winter (November–March).
- Experiences are child-centred and can spread over several days.
- Three hours of contact is spread over indoors (1 hour) and outdoors (2 hours).
- Toddlers spend a portion of their day outside, both in the morning and the afternoon.

Transitional spaces:

- Preschool children are dropped off by parents or caregivers in the Garden area.
- Afterschool care for grades K–4 (ages 4–9 years) begins outside and moves indoors when it gets dark.

DOP 6:1 expresses the movement and outcomes of learning that are goals for all the children who attend Acorn Learning Center. Through nurture, intentional activities, consultations with children and their families, and using the outdoor rooftop garden, our intent is to assist each child in becoming engaged, aware, caring and active.

We attend to four areas or domains of development: physical, cognitive, social/emotional, and spiritual. Each area can be distinct in its movement. For example, each one has:

(a) an internal 'inside' growth area (the small arrow), that moves to
(b) an outer growth area or concept 'outside' (the middle arrow), and that moves to
(c) a wider growth area 'beyond' (the longest arrow).

Each area overlaps in many ways. Growth of one domain is embedded in the growth of the others. For example, a cognitively engaged child is curious about the world around them. In the same way, a spiritually caring child is full of wonder and awe in the natural world around them. Another example is a socially/emotionally aware child who moves from self-awareness to an awareness of the 'other', which brings about a sense

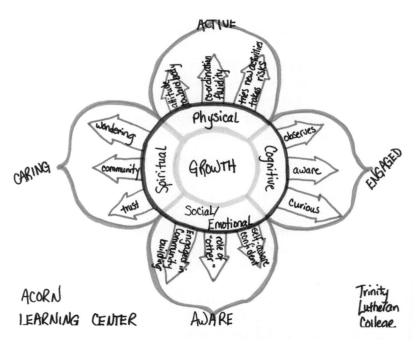

DOP 6:1 *Diagram of Practice to share the values and behaviours the authors are developing*

of community. Along with that, a physically active child tries new things, taking calculated risks, both physically and socially.

DOP 6:1 is designed to be a flowering plant, indicating the emphasis on out of doors as the primary environment for growth.

CASE STUDY TWO

Name: Auchlone Nature Kindergarten

Location: Perthshire, Scotland, UK

Type of setting: A Nature Kindergarten where 90–100 per cent of the time is spent outside, all year round, in temperatures that range from -15 degrees to 30 degrees Celsius. Core age range is 2–5 years, for 48 weeks a year, and opening times are 8.30am–5.30pm. There are additional programmes for 5–11 year olds: John Muir award, Forest School and residential camps with community programmes through the charity Living Classrooms. The site has two types of forest, a loch and stream, which are linked to general areas such as the vegetable patch, mud kitchen and chicken coop in the outdoor area.

The vision and values of the centre and the experiences across the forest site are represented in the graphic of the Thistle, the national flower of Scotland. The words have been chosen carefully, and are included in the paragraph below to raise awareness of the way we live by our values.

The vision and values of Auchlone:

- Place: The gatehouse (built in 1854) is rooted in a strong sense of place. The stone house and an open-fronted kinder kitchen are the indoor spaces. The background is an ancient tartan from our location – the Abercairny Estate. Traditionally made from natural plant dyes, it holds the colours of the place in a pattern that reflects the interwoven nature of people, place and land that create our community. This gives the team a sense of gravitas as being part of a cultural community with families. Many families have a real connection to the cultural community, but need to travel from outside our physical community for up to 1.5 hours.
- Values of love, hope and justice underpin our nature pedagogy across the inside, outside and beyond.
- We support learning dispositions which cross over traditional curriculum divisions. These underpin the Curriculum for Excellence (3–18 years) that we follow in Scotland. The words at the top of DOP 6:2 are the eight words we feel most strongly about. They stem from our sense of justice that children have rights from birth, one of which is a right to nature, which in turn supports the development of further dispositions:

  ○ Freedom – the right to have a childhood full of engaging experiences that fulfil all the human needs we have.
  ○ Consultation – the right to have a voice through being fully involved in the planning through Floorbooks™.
  ○ Motivation – the right to joyful moments that inspire and connect.
  ○ Awe – the right to have experiences that support a sense of connection to nature.
  ○ Wonderment – the right to have time to just be, full of curiosity and engagement with the natural world.
  ○ Empowerment – the right to share in the life of a centre as a valued part of that community.
  ○ Respect for each other and themselves.
  ○ Care – the right to be in a loving environment that supports them to feel cherished and unique.

DOP 6:3 (see also DOP 5:1) shares the thinking we have been engaged in as a team, to consider the way that our children engage with the three distinct areas. The inside space is calm, with gentle colours and home-like features, such as a fireplace and stove, and divided play areas for creativity and writing, which have become more integrated and more home-like. Some areas have disappeared (such as indoor sand) as the team spend more time outside. The inside environments now support the outside, rather than the other way round. Our journey is recorded on Standards and Quality Development Plans or Centre Improvement Plans and in a graphical form in a Continuum Book. Children's ideas are taken from the Floorbooks™ (see Chapter 5), and parents' ideas are gathered through our Communication Book, which records parent and carer voices which can then be integrated into plans.

There are many transitional areas that support children to create links in learning, such as window displays, but also larger physical areas, such as the 'Meeting Turtle' or the 'Dark Den'. These areas are locations where children hesitate and gather, often without prompting. Dips and hollows, and points of elevation, are scattered over the site both inside the smaller area and beyond. The home-made gate, arches and piles of stones give messages about transitions that children read very clearly.

Buildings have also had a role in supporting physical, intellectual and emotional transitions. Children's experience of darkness led the team to consider the learning pathways between our spaces and how we could use time, resources and adult interaction and planning to explore darkness. The 'Dark Shelter' is not only a drop-off space for parents to settle and chat, but also

DOP 6:2   *Poster of the values that underpin practice*

an area for cosy candlelit stories. Children sit around the fire near the kinder kitchen at dusk to build up their ability to see at night. Then the lights in the buildings can be dimmed so that the intensity of darkness increases and we can see the stars. Groups can stay up at the Firehouse at dusk in the winter and then walk with lanterns back to the centre. This gentle development of confidence, skill and resilience is achieved through transitioning, with mindfulness and understanding of prior experiences across the inside to outside and then beyond.

Children move in different ways around the three spaces. The wilder areas seem to support a sense of wandering or exploration and meandering that is not as apparent in the outdoor play area. There are a few key paths that are purposeful journeys with a set preparation of packing up, setting off and arriving. These journey routes change each year with each group, with set meeting places such as the 'Singing Tree' or the 'Tree with a Window'.

The learning dispositions, such as courage and curiosity, perseverance, trust, responsibility, and confidence, interweave with skills and behaviours that we see in nature, such as climbing, settling, anticipating, decision-making, hiding, resting, looking, being, listening. These happen all over the site. Some features of the natural landscape give an intuitive message to children that stimulates a behaviour or action. Elevations and depressions encourage settling, certain large canopy trees encourage resting and reflecting, intersections of pathways encourage meetings, enclosed areas support settlement, with a mud kitchen, for example. Boundaries and entrances are marked by arches and waymarkers.

The process of creating graphics to think helped us to self-evaluate our practice.

We noted where behaviours were taking place; we had conversations about what time, space and resource use looked like for us; we discussed our role, and especially, used the diagram on adult positioning to consider our confidence to give children space. We have always planned over three spaces, but have now created an improved diagram of the possibilities to share with visitors and parents.

The integration of multiple learning spaces in terms of learning is key to the engagement of the children from 2–5 years old. The intentionality of the learning is threaded across at least 4–5 outdoor and indoor spaces (see also DOP 5:1).

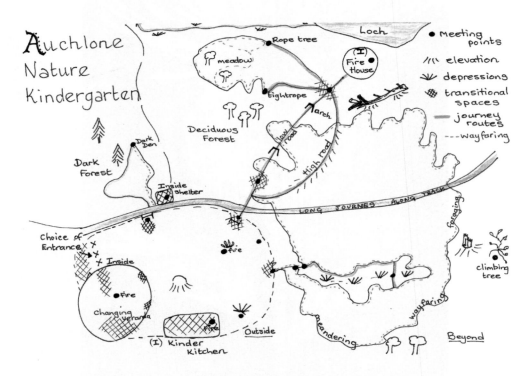

DOP 6:3 *Diagram of Practice to show play behaviours, the link inside and outside and into the beyond*

The learning pathways

The circular diagram here in this case study tracks the concepts/skills and knowledge of learning as the children's fascinations move across the physical boundaries of the indoor space (which is a 19th century cottage) to the outdoor area (the kinder kitchen, garden and small wood) to the spaces beyond (a variety of different types of broadleaf and coniferous forest with a small loch).

The process was undertaken as part of an action research cycle to consider where most of the nodes of learning take place. The phrase 'node of learning', is chosen to reflect that there are points where the learning pathways intersect or branch. They are often provocations structured by the adult with a clear learning intention. The intention can be linked to curriculum coverage, skill, knowledge or concepts. Not all of our planning should be adult structured, so the node allows there to be possible lines of development that spin away from it in a variety of ways that children lead.

The children were exploring the concept of growth and the forest was full of ferns starting to unfurl. The team drew the diagram and it shows the movement and links in learning from the forest (B) to the outside (O) and to the indoor spaces (I).

The planning grids for Auchlone take into account the three spaces we work within to support the team to give value to learning in all the spaces, even though it is presented in a different way.

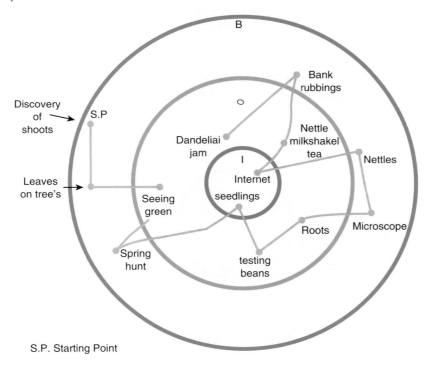

Tracking the movement of the learning pathway and key nodes of learning

Inside	Outside	Beyond
Exploration of semi-transparency on light box	**Lying down to explore leaves** (semi-opaque and opaque)	**Starting point: Growth of fern and other plants in the forest**
'Changing from brown to green' Seed growth from brown seeds to green	**Seeing 'green'** **Being still to notice**	Photography of nature waking up **Spring hunting**
Planting seedlings in earth pots	Protecting new growth with fences	Transient art using different leaves
Exploration of the variety of beans to sort	**Tasting beans**	Cooking bean stew on the open fire
Shapes of leaves puzzle	**Digging in the garden to find roots**	**Looking at roots under the tree with hand held microscopes**

Inside	Outside	Beyond
Sorting real leaves	Making nettle milkshake	**Gathering nettles**
Research recipes on the internet	Collecting dandelions from lawn	Clearing spaces of leaves for shoots to have some light
Transient art of dandelions, leaves	**Cooking dandelion jam in the kinder kitchen**	Making mixtures

The bold writing shows the nodes of learning and the other boxes share the possible lines of development that come from those moments or from the children directly. This grid is to share the balance of the adult structure with the other opportunities available to children to access as they wish to demonstrate the co-constructivism of our approach to teaching and learning.

The adult role at Auchlone

The last set of diagrams has been created by the team at Auchlone as part of their reflexive practice within our philosophy of nature pedagogy. The team come from a variety of backgrounds that stem from their love of being outside. The team have the support to develop their skills and knowledge through graduate courses in teaching and early years practice. The special nature of working in an outdoor setting has been supported with continuous professional development at a 5 day intensive in the summer time. The use of Floorbooks™ (Warden 2006) as a form of planning is linked to learning with nature through the Journeys into Nature course and the One Award Nature Kindergarten Level 3 that were written by the author. The values and virtues guide the practice in Auchlone. The emphasis for training is to explore how to empower the staff to take ownership for their decisions, so that interactions and relationships come through as the key aspects of our early years practice.

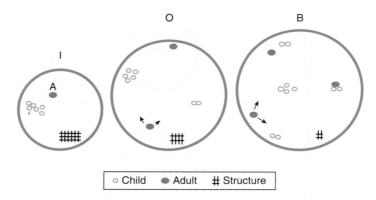

| ○ Child | ● Adult | # Structure |

Reflection on the place of the adult role in outdoor learning

Inside the cottage (I)

- More structured; resources in areas for learning.
- Groups of children play in smaller spaces.
- Closer intentional adult contact framed by areas of learning.

Outside in the kinder kitchen and the garden forest (O)

- Less structure; central resource area.
- Distant contact with adult for supervision.
- Free flow inside and outside.
- Shared supervision – one key observer of outdoor area.

Beyond in the forest (B)

- Little or no structure; found natural resources.
- Pockets of children in chosen spaces.
- Close emotional contact as children seek it.
- Close interaction/awareness of whole team with one main observer of the site.

The environment is constantly evolving as the thinking processes change within the adult team and the children that we work with. The values and virtues are the solid threads that hold our practice together. The process of reflection and reflexivity allow the team to create new understandings of our practice that are set within our culture, in our space and within our time.

CASE STUDY THREE

Name: Cowgate Under 5's Centre

Location: Edinburgh, Scotland, UK

Type of setting: A local authority Early Years centre. Children can attend 52 weeks a year, from 8am to 5.45pm. Children range from 6 months to 5 years. The children have continual access to a natural outdoor area and access to the Forest School for six half-day sessions. Children also go on Stevie's minibus to Stickland, which is a short drive away.

The centre is rooted in Froebel's philosophy. Froebel was a German pedagogue (1782–1852), a student of Pestalozzi, who laid the foundation for modern education based on the recognition that children have unique needs and capabilities. He created the concept of the 'kindergarten' and the educational resources known as Froebel Gifts.

The centre's growth can be traced from the transformation of the outside area, to the use of Johnstone Terrace Forest School, and then to the increased use of the Stickland Nature Kindergarten site (see Chapter 4 for the Standards and Quality Improvement Plan and Poster).

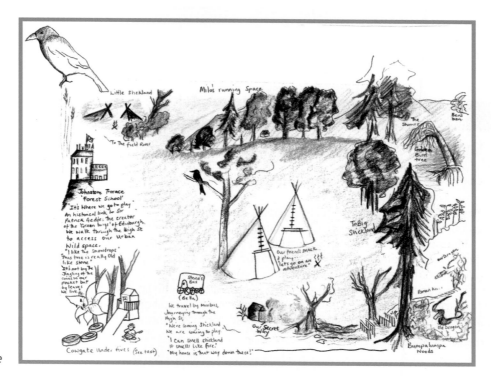

Mapping the outdoor space

The map of the area above shows the different spaces to which the children have access. Mapping with the children allows the adult to be mindful of the spaces that hold significance for them. 'Milo's running space' and 'Ben's den' illustrate that sensitive attunement.

Adult reflection on the experience states:

> The children spend long un-interrupted time within nature, playing, exploring alone or with friends. Over time, we have observed our children's innate connection with nature. The children have travelled and mapped the site. Using all of their senses, they have encountered deep snow, thunderstorms, rain, mist, ice and wind. The play is very imaginative, integrating urban experiences encountered on the way to the forest site, or brought out by experiences at home, for example, 'Bumpalumpa'.

DOP 6.4 was made to show the links that children make from home to the centre and across multiple environments. These include children's voices, adult reflection and parental engagement in an holistic image.

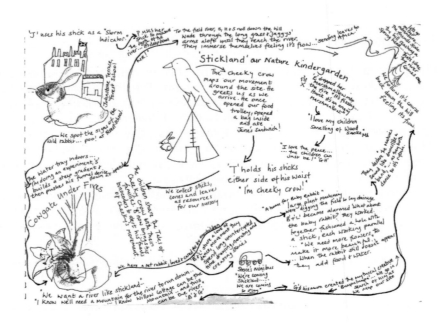

DOP 6:4   *Diagram of Practice*

CASE STUDY FOUR

Name: Forest School (7–19 years)

Location: Shropshire, England, UK

Type of setting: This school is a specialist independent, residential school for boys aged 7–19 years. It is situated in a rural landscape with a Forest School and camp nearby.

   The school accepts referrals from mainstream education establishments. The pupils can no longer successfully access mainstream education, despite the best efforts of the special educational needs (SEN) provision in that setting.

   The school accepts pupils with a diagnosis of Autistic Spectrum Disorder, together with Asperger's syndrome and a range of co-morbid conditions. There are 59 pupils on the roll, including a combination of day boys, weekly boarders and 52-week placements.

The school follows the National Curriculum up to GCSE level and runs a timetabled day for the pupils who are in tutor groups, of which four students is the average number.

In 2005, I began to consider alternatives to the built education environment. It was clear to me that many of the behaviour issues that were occurring in the built learning environment could be dealt with, or at least ameliorated, in a more natural setting.

It is evident that many issues are related to a breakdown in communication. Skills which we take for granted are, in the autistic mind, missing threads in the complex tapestry of interpersonal communication. As this tapestry cannot be unpicked, the challenges surrounding successful communication are lifelong.

This realisation encouraged me to seek a way to provide a setting where communication strategies could be developed. When used correctly, these strategies would enable successful communication in key areas of interaction between the student and range of other non-autistic people.

This could be in an area as simple as ordering a cup of coffee, something a non-autistic person would not think twice about, but would quickly exhaust one of our students. The range of options and choices of style type (topping, for example) would quickly lead to a mental overload, as one failed set of communication collides with the next, and with frustration and anger kicking in to destroy the interaction.

I therefore looked to nature. We set up a Forest School in a 30-acre wood and, after some difficulties, obtained one full day and one half day, which were embedded into the curriculum. We have a rolling programme of year groups passing through, so that now, after eight years, every pupil in the school from the juniors to the Year 11s, have experienced learning in nature on a regular basis. We also spend a week of every year living under canvas in an area of Scottish woodland, where in-depth work over a protracted period provides the opportunity to make real progress.

The key elements of sound, colour and shape were examined and compared to the built learning environment. Within the built environment, sound can be a major problem due to the heightened sensory awareness of the ASD (Autistic Spectrum Disorders) student – chairs grate, rooms echo, lights click and hum continually, and doors bang. Colours are monotone and uniform and shapes are angular, rigid and hard. These elements, combined in a classroom setting, together with the pressure of time, can heighten levels of anxiety and tension and hinder the process of communication, as the brain is processing so much negative input that the construction process required to formulate responses breaks down into negative behaviour.

The natural environment has the opposite effect. We have noted that pupils' levels of arousal drop as they transit the winding path through the woods, and the natural sound and landscape permeate their senses. They become gradually aware of the Forest School camp through the woods, and their attention is drawn into the kinaesthetic process of gathering and chopping the wood for the cooking fire. The fire is lit and a common object is achieved, which is to draw everyone into the fire's circle and engage them with the nature around them.

Kinaesthetic tasks, which are small and achievable, combined with the natural setting, provide a platform on which we build the communication strategies. The mind is engaged with the hands and not focused on constructing responses.

As the task progresses, responses flow more easily. A need for assistance to achieve a personal aim gives opportunities to interact with peers and use a series of statements which will fulfil that need and therefore be reused away from the Forest School environment. All of this is facilitated by the team of trained instructors who have a common goal for the students engaged in the session.

Do we use nature for learning? Absolutely. The learning process for our students is centred on their presence in nature, bringing them to a level of awareness by reducing the sensory irritation they encounter in the built environment. This allows them to function kinaesthetically, without the constraints of timetables and the tyranny of the clock. It is what they take from their time in the forest that enables them to engage in successful communication strategies in the 'outside world'. Having faith in the success of the communication 'scaffold' they have discovered, students trust and use them more often, allowing their journeys to the 'outside' to be made without stress and with confidence, so they will be understood.

The use of graphics

This process of analysis really highlighted the process I have attempted to outline above. It enabled me to visualise the flow of experiences from the built environment, to the woods and on into the wider aspect of our yearly week in Scotland. It also enabled me to visualise how these experiences built scaffolds into the outside world. The team created DOP 6:5 to explain the importance of every part of the Forest School experience.

In an educational environment, where familiarity with the benefits of learning with nature is not uniform, it has supported collegiate understanding of the principle of learning with nature, rather than just about it. It has been a thought-provoking process.

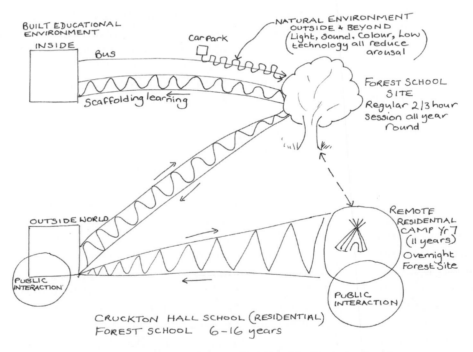

DOP 6:5   *Diagram of Practice: To share the 'scaffolding' in Forest school*

CASE STUDY FIVE

Name: Hval Gård Barnehage

Location: Muncipallity of Asker, Oslo, Norway

Type of setting: Hval Gård Barnehage is a Nature Kindergarten with a 'wild' outdoor area of forest and sea. Sami-inspired wooden huts (single pole tents from the Sami people of Lapland) are located within the 'base camp' area. The huts have no electricity and the ovens and open fires supply the warmth and cooking facilities. There are several inland lakes and the Oslofjord is nearby, offering boating activities as part of the outdoor learning experience for children aged 4–5 years.

*Transition spaces allow
children to make decisions*

*Children explore
land- and water-
based experiences*

In Hval Gård Barnehage, we never use the word *tur-dag*, which means an excursion day, especially for activities outside the kindergarten, because, for us, every day is a *tur-dag*. We don't mind if it is raining, snowing or windy outside. All the children are used to dressing up for any kind of weather or temperatures, and they are almost never ill. In this process of learning, the children have to be allowed to experiment themselves, so as to feel the difference in temperature and moisture. They need to find out for themselves what the appropriate item of clothing is for wearing in these different conditions.

Our kindergarten has a rural setting just on the outskirts of a small wood and is close to the seaside. We use the nearby fjord with our own boats both to go to the nearby small islands and to catch fish, crabs and mussels. Lunch is prepared on open fires and eaten outdoors, and often consists of what we find and can use in the nature around us, such as fresh fish that is prepared on an open fire and caught by the children themselves. Can you imagine anything better? The days go by in a 'relaxed mood', with baking, fishing and hiking, for example. We usually let the children decide where to go and what to do. Inside the boat we can read books, tell stories, play games with words and numbers, sing and tell jokes, even if it is a rainy day. We can also start the process of working with our 3D maps and our Floorbooks™, which we take with us between spaces, and these are transported with the rest of the tools we need. The children work on their ideas on the boat and when they return to the small huts at our base camp, within the kindergarten.

Transition spaces such as the dock allow us to prepare in many ways

We use a lot of the inland lakes, both in summer and wintertime as seen in DOP 6: 6. In the summer, we go and study different birds, insects in the water, or we fish in the traditional way with just a rod and a hook. It is exciting to follow the stream that goes down to the lake, and there is even a waterfall, where we can creep in and watch from behind the 'water curtain'. In wintertime, it all freezes solid, and you can actually climb the frozen waterfall. The lake also freezes, and it is great fun to go ice-skating, when you can actually watch everything that happens in the water underneath you. We drill holes to do ice-fishing and you can see the fish catching the bait.

When the snow comes, we can go skiing across the lakes and experiment with kites and sails to see how the wind can be used as the power that pushes us forward.

We see a lot of creativity among the children. They are not accustomed to having toys with them as they go into the woods, and therefore are used to playing or creating things with what they can find. The image below shows a boy who started drawing gnomes in the small bubbles on the rocky seashore that appears when it is a low tide. Nature helps them to soon learn that they have to cooperate to find the best solutions for how to deal with different experiments, and that it is more fun playing together than alone.

I truly believe that the time spent in our nature kindergarten is in many ways giving the children a headstart. The physical health of these children is high, the ability to cooperate increases, and their ever-experimenting minds are stretched by the possibilities.

Creativity in nature

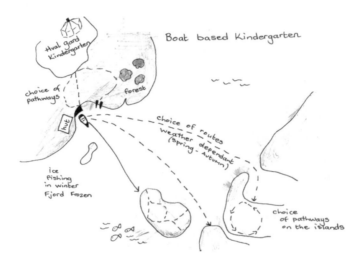

DOP 6:6   *Map of the wayfaring and journeys*

Inside areas are located throughout the forest

Creating a diagram of practice helps us to vocalise and define the way we feel about nature. For us, there are real boundaries in nature – a high cliff or a deep river. Some adults put up boundaries like fences that are not real for the child. A fence does not help a child to learn, but all the challenges and natural limitations of nature do. Our inside space is designed to support everything we do outside as shown in DOP 6:7. They have no heating but the use of fire has a function and a purpose for learning.

Diagrams of Practice allow others to see the intentional way in which we think of a nature kindergarten rather than any other model. We work with nature in a relaxed, unhurried way – all day, every day.

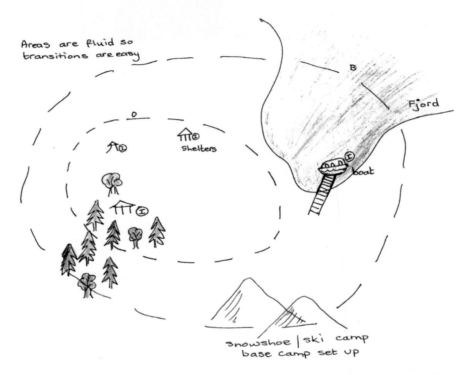

DOP 6:7   *To show multiple 'inside' spaces set within outdoor areas and spaces beyond*

CASE STUDY SIX

Name: Sault College Child Development Centre

Location: Sault Ste Marie, Ontario, Canada

Type of setting: A Lab school for the college's Early Childhood Education Programme. On-campus childcare services that accommodate children from 18 months to 5 years. It provides a licensed early learning programme for the students and staff of the college. Our licensed Child Development Centre is staffed by qualified Early Childhood Educators who are assisted by students. There are several 'wild' spaces within walking distance, including a wooded area, located behind the centre.

Springing Forward: a trial project

We planned a trial programme in the late spring of 2013 for eight of the 24 children (2.5–4 years) from our regular licensed preschool room. Finding a natural area proved to be a challenge, but we finally found a location that was close to the building – a large, secluded snow bank, providing us with our own sheltered 'wild' space.

During our two-week trial outdoors, we were provided with many unique learning experiences. For example, the children learned about the states of water (ice, snow, slush and water) by observing the daily changes in the puddles they played in. With the coming of spring, the children had many opportunities to observe the seasonal changes unfolding daily in the flora and fauna that trigger traditions in the community, such as maple syruping.

Toys were not made available and were not requested. We were amazed at how engaged the children were in this ever-changing environment and the learning outcomes it provided. We saw examples of how their developmental skills were being extended beyond a knowledge of the natural world. There were many examples of cooperative play, where the children worked together and helped one another. Gross and fine motor skills were enhanced, and opportunities to share their stories arose. Children were problem-solving and thinking creatively, especially with the open-ended play opportunities that the wilder natural space provided. They also displayed enthusiasm and a sense of pride and accomplishment as they engaged in challenging and meaningful work, such as pulling wagons, putting up and taking down the tarpaulins, and climbing large snow banks.

Over the course of our trial, we noticed a huge change in the children's sense of pride, responsibility and collaborative work with others. The daily transport of supplies to and from the woods was clear evidence of this shift.

The change in the emotional climate which flowed over from our outdoor space to our regular programme environments was unexpected. We observed that indoors some of the children frequently showed frustration, anger and a reluctance to try new things, and play was often aimless and unfocused. The indoor environment often felt busy, overwhelming and loud. Different strategies were employed, such as reducing group size and increasing time in the gym hall, but these had little effect. This changed when we ventured into our 'wild' space. The physical area provided each child with more space and constant variability, as well as the opportunity to find a quiet place when they wanted to spend time alone.

We noticed that on the first day, children were looking for permission to engage in activities such as climbing the mountain of snow or stepping into the puddles. Once they realised that they could explore quite freely, they engaged in familiar and new experiences for long periods of time – something we felt they probably didn't get to do very often. When the children went outside, there seemed to be more time and space for uninterrupted play.

It was evident that their self-confidence began to blossom as they engaged in meaningful daily tasks, and their sense of accomplishment and pride showed in their beaming faces when they had completed their tasks. Linked to this was the change in their interactions with one another. Children were more attentive, and responded when others enthusiastically wanted to show them their discoveries. We noted that there was less conflict and more cooperative play.

A significant change occurred in one of the children who had been identified as being on the autism spectrum. The outdoor space met the needs for high sensorial experiences, which were not always met in the indoor setting, or were disruptive to the programme. We found that once those needs were met in our 'wild' space, the child discovered new ways to meet those needs in the indoor and playground settings. We also noted that the child was more attentive for longer periods of time outdoors, which also carried over into the regular environment.

As educators, we changed too. Initially apprehensive, we began to develop a comfort level where we trusted that children were competent and capable, and we learned to respect their instincts. We continued to ensure that the children were safe, and noticed that our more relaxed states filtered down to the children. We also had more time to engage with them in meaningful conversations, and had the time to observe and document their learning.

The 'wild' space seemed to be an impetus that affected us all; the children were more confident, content and engaged, and we felt more relaxed in this natural environment. On returning to our indoor setting, these changes stayed with us. And what was most astonishing was that this change seemed to radiate outwards, changing the emotional climate in both the indoor and outdoor environments. We are convinced that a nature-based programme can have a positive influence, not only in an outdoor setting, but also on indoor and playground environments, for both children and practitioners:

> Our experience in creating the Diagrams of Practice made us think differently about the impact of our short, trial, nature-based programme. At first, we wanted to focus on the learning pathways of concepts and curriculum. Through our discussions, we realised that we were most impacted by the influence of nature in changing the emotional climate of our environments. (Angela Dawson, Practitioner)

> Through creating the diagrams, I learned that, although we all originally seemed to have different ideas about what was most significant, we all felt strongly about the impact on the change in the emotional climate of our programme. It sparked an interesting brainstorming session and was a great way to start a conversation. (Candace Boston, Practitioner)

> It was challenging to think outside the box in this way. It's something I don't normally do. It felt good to be 'stretched', and it triggered some different thought processes. I think it makes our thinking more visible. (Andrea Welz, Practitioner)

Experiencing the joy of splashing through a puddle

*Children being part of
the team creating base camp*

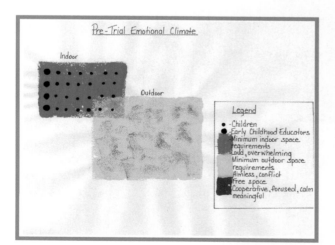
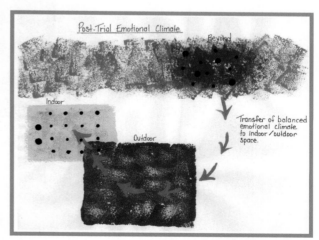

Sharing pedagogical thinking through a Diagram of Practice

CASE STUDY SEVEN

Name: Sooke Nature Kindergarten

Location: Sooke School District, Southern Vancouver Island, Canada

Type of setting: A pilot programme for a Nature Kindergarten in its second year and based at Sangster Elementary School for 4–5 year olds. Initially, the children spend a half-day in the morning in natural settings, including a forest space. One of the aims is to develop physical and mental health and foster deep connections with nature to support social and emotional learning, with strong ties to the community. A focus on 'Aboriginal ways of knowing', with input from local Aboriginal organisations, is part of their ethos.

DOP 6:8 *Diagram of Practice to share the holistic nature of the Nature Kindergarten*

We made two photos of the children by a great and grand tree that sits at the centre of the diagram (DOP 6:8). We then created branches of a tree. The nest was the educators' journey and has the words:

- partnership, collaboration, connection, new ideas, fluid, flexible, connection to place, in tune, improvisational, relationships.

The spider web in the branches is the children's journey and has the words:

- traditional narratives, connected on many levels, awareness, spiritual, relationships, nature, uneven surfaces, sense of place ... connected, strength and coordination, awareness, community, play, inseparable.

The roots are the community engagement:

- waldkindegarten, Iur och skur, sharing ideas locally, slow thoughtful process, diverse expertise, innovation, school district support, resources.

The rock is family support:

- acceptance of dirt and risk, greater connection to nature, traditional learnings, seeing children as learners/teachers, comfort in rain and cold, advocates, realise children's capabilities.

The sun is our pedagogical principles:

- Connecting deeply with nature through play.
- Physical/mental health.
- Traditional/local ways of knowing and understanding.
- Learning collaboratively as part of an empathetic community.
- The environment as co-teacher.

CASE STUDY EIGHT

Name: Spirit of Play

Location: Denmark, Western Australia

Type of setting: Community School that caters for children aged 3–7, including a preschool playgroup and home-schooled children aged 3–14 years from the local community. The school follows a nature-based pedagogy, where learning is mainly outdoors in the surrounding bush river and beach sites, or with natural materials in the classroom and playground.

Our setting is one of great natural beauty, with tall Karri and Jarrah forests enfolding the school building and the picturesque Denmark (or Kwoorabup), a river flowing into the wide Wilson inlet, immediately across the road from our site. Our climate is mild and cool for Australia, with warm dry summers and wet winters. Our wider environment consists mainly of regrowth forests and green pasturelands used for cattle and dairy farms.

The traditional owners of this country were the Noongar people and, more specifically, the Kwoorabup River marked the boundary between the Minang and Bibulmun peoples, who formed two of the many dialect groups of the wider Noongar nation. Colonisation of this country took place between the late 1890s and early 1900s, with the widespread felling of timber in the region. Little has been written about the impact of this industry on the Noongar people but by 1913 there were very few families left.

(Continued)

(Continued)

A core part of the ethos of Spirit of Play Community School is the reconnection of the Denmark community with the traditional language and culture of the Indigenous, Noongar people. This is made possible through the help of key Indigenous facilitators and Elders from Denmark and the surrounding Minang and Bibulmun regions. The children all learn to speak the Noongar language and to understand the human relationship with Boodja (country) through storytelling, song and bush craft sessions. The following case study provides an example of the connections children have made between the initial teachings of the Indigenous Elders and their own lives, as they continue to explore the myriad possibilities suggested by stories enacted as play.

Building koornts

The koornt, a traditional Noongar bush hut, is a simple conical or tepee-like structure made of branches used as the shelter and sleeping place for a small family, with an open doorway in which a fire would be built. Larry Blight, a local Indigenous facilitator, came and showed us how to design and build a koornt.

The koornt was constructed from a main frame of interlocking branches, cloaked in tea-tree (melaleuca sap) brush to repel rain.

A more simple structure was built by a 6-year-old child using the same principles as for the original koornt.

The picture that shows a 'koomal' house shaped like a koornt was drawn by an 8-year-old girl.

After the session, the children were engaged for many weeks, not only playing within the newly constructed koornt, but in creating their own shelters from bush materials. The idea of a home, a place where they could shelter and belong to, came through strongly for the children in their explorations of these structures. Some of the expressions of this were games involving dancing round the koornt with clapsticks, seasonal hunting and foraging expeditions, collecting bush medicines for minor injuries, and ceremonial activities, such as crushing ochre and using this for face painting, and which brought to life for them traditional living. These explorations took place within the classroom, in the playground (where the koornt was built) and also in our designated bush places, where the children will now inevitably decide to 'build a koornt' in order to create a 'home space' for their play. Further explorations have taken the shape of creating shelters for various bush creatures and fairy-folk.

After learning about the stick nests that the 'koomals' (brush-tailed possum) create, the children made a koomal koornt in the playground.

Two 7-year-old girls created the 'fairy koornt' using moss as the outer cladding.

Over the course of the year, these structures became the focus for many games in the playground, and children spontaneously adjusted their dwellings to more practical designs as their games progressed. Important considerations included how to keep the inside dry when it rained and how to create enough space for a family to sleep.

The children's growing understanding of the Noongar way of life continues to be enriched through our understanding of the connection that exists between ourselves, our community and our Boodja (country).

Our experience in creating the Diagram of Practice as seen in DOP 6:9 was an opportunity to rediscover our shared passion for our school and that, despite the tasks that tend to overwhelm us on a day-to-day level, there is a core vision that brings us together. It also reminded us that our work is part of a greater context of a global movement towards reconnecting children with the environment. We would like to acknowledge the Noongar and the Widgella

Community building

Small-scale koornt

(non-Indigenous) communities and their ancestors for continuing to share their love and knowledge of the land (boodjah):

> There is the possibility of changing the destructive habits of our society through opening our hearts to this land. (Zoe Car, parent and school council member)

> How enriched my teaching has become by the connection I have to country. I recognise that this all has a purpose to me – it is not just a meaningless curriculum. (Regi Peppin, Practitioner)

A koomal house shaped like a koornt

Fairy koornt

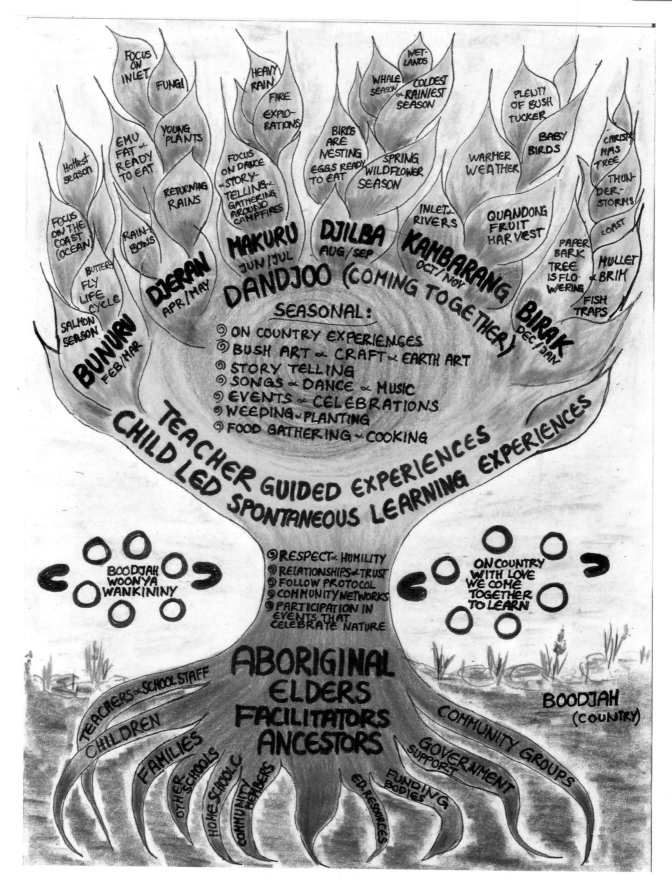

DOP 6:9 *Diagram of Practice: To share philosophy*

CASE STUDY NINE

Name: Stretch the Imagination

Location: San Francisco, California, USA

Type of setting: An urban preschool that caters for 4–5 year olds. Centrally located in San Francisco, the setting is housed in an historic Victorian home with an adjacent back yard space. There is a national park within the city limits that offers a forest space for the children for one school day per week.

Name: The Way of the Dinosaurs

One of our core values is connecting children with nature. Once a week, rain or shine, our children spend their school day in a national park called The Presidio, and do not come to the school building. The intention is to explore and experience nature with links to our project work that take place back at school.

During our 2011–2012 school year, a group of ten pre-kindergarten children (4–5 years) embarked on a journey that took them deeper into the forest and into an understanding of the power of technology. This particular group of children had been exploring the forest for three years, so they were well acquainted with the secret places, well-travelled paths and all that the forest had to offer. One day, the children noticed a giant tree they had not seen before. This tree soon became a destination of interest. After 'bush whacking' their way down the hill, they encountered what they soon named 'The Sweetie Tree'. Large leafy branches cascaded to the ground, creating a full canopy of protection with many limbs to climb, and the surrounding trees creating tunnels to explore. They returned to The Sweetie Tree weekly, and these settings, along with the surrounding forest, soon became the backdrop for new worlds and elaborate fantasy play.

The children were fascinated with storytelling and had spent many of their afternoons back at school exploring this craft and creating their own tales. Each child would take to the stage for their own show, often inviting peers to join in as characters in their narrative. The storytelling carried over into their days in the forest, and soon an elaborate, group story called 'The Way of the Dinosaurs' was developing. The children decided they wanted to shoot a film so that their parents could see the stories from their time in the forest. Over the course of five months, these ten children wrote, directed and produced their own film. From this project, two main committees emerged: the Mapping Committee and the Movie Committee. The Mapping Committee was tasked with creating a detailed map of the forest landmarks so that those who viewed the movie could then visit the forest and trace the Dinosaurs' path. The Mapping Committee children were also cast in the film as characters. The Movie Committee wrote the final story, and then cast, narrated and filmed the movie in the forest with their friends. In the final three months of the school year, the children helped to create the costumes and props, and all were featured in the film.

Parents also became actively involved in helping during certain key points in the project. They taught the children the skill of sewing, so that they could make their own costumes. The artist-in-residence, who specialised in clay, and the skills she taught the children allowed them to create important set props, including the dinosaur bones and eggs.

While the children visited the forest more often as their project work developed, they could not spend every school day in the forest. It soon became important to bring the forest back into our classrooms, and technology became a key tool in practising their scenes back at school. They started by projecting photographs of the key areas from the forest onto the studio walls with an overhead projector. Shadow acting became an important part of their process, allowing the forest to come alive inside the school walls and in the back yard. Loud roaring and stomping could be heard throughout the school and our willow hut outside soon came to house the precious dinosaur eggs.

Over time, the children took ownership of the school camera to film their own scenes in the forest. This footage was then projected onto the wall back at school, and at their first screening there was audible excitement as they came to understand the power of video.

Over the next two months, they actively shot and re-shot scenes in the forest based on their story. They branched out into other areas of the forest and filmed their final ocean scenes at a spring. Their story ends as the dinosaurs travel down the spring 'well' to where they still live today: at the bottom of the ocean.

In five short months, these young children wrote, cast and narrated their own film, stimulated by their connection to a 'wild' space. They created all the props and sewed all their own costumes using recycled fabric and materials. They acted, directed, and filmed their movie with the guidance and final editing skills of their two teachers. When the final cut was shown on graduation day, the children had completed a 14-minute short film, which was screened for all their parents and family members. In addition to the screening, the children provided a detailed map for all those who wanted to retrace the dinosaurs' journey.

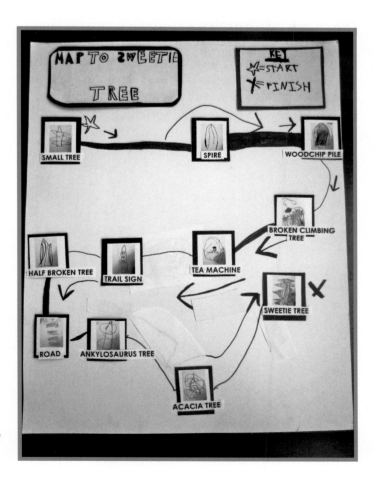

Children's sense of place created through mapping

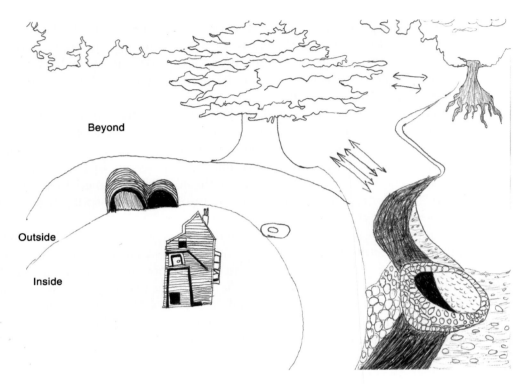

Beyond

Outside

Inside

DOP 6:10   *Diagram of Practice: To show connected spaces*

Diagram of Practice

The process of drawing the journey of the children in DOP 6: 10 really pulled out to the team the connection we have between inside, outside and the wilder natural spaces around us. The Presidio Forest is now seen as an integral part of our environment rather than simply a place to visit, and it was the film technology that really brought all the elements together in this connected experience for children, staff and families.

Bibliography

ALLIN, L. & HUMBERSTONE, B. 2010. Introducing 'Journey(s)' in adventure and outdoor learning research. *Journal of Adventure Education & Outdoor Learning*, 10, 71–75.

ARGYRIS, C. & SCHÖN, D. 1978. *Organizational Learning: A Theory of Action Perspective*. Reading, MA: Addison Wesley.

ARNOLD, C. and THE PEN GREEN TEAM. 2010. *Understanding Schemas and Emotion in Early Childhood*. London: Sage.

ASSOCIATION of INDEPENDENT SCHOOLS of WESTERN AUSTRALIA (AISWA). 2015. *Nature Pedagogy: Case Studies of School Development*. Perth: AISWA.

ATHEY, C. 1990. *Extending Thought in Young Children*. London: Paul Chapman.

BAINES, E., BLATCHFORD, P. & KUTNICK, P. 2003. Changes in grouping practices over primary and secondary school. *International Journal of Educational Research*, 39, 9–34.

BALL, D., GILL, T. & SPIEGAL, B. 2008. *Managing Risk in Play Provision: Implementation Guide*. Nottingham: DCSF (Department for Children, Schools and Families).

BARONE, T. E. & EISNER, E. W. 2011. *Arts Based Research*. Thousand Oaks, CA: SAGE.

BEAMES, S. 2002. The black box. *Pathways: The Ontario Journal of Outdoor Education*, 14 (Autumn), 35.

BEAMES, S., HIGGINS, P.J. & NICOL, R. 2011. *Learning Outside the Classroom: Theory and Guidelines for Practice*. Abingdon: Taylor & Francis.

BERINGER, A. & MARTIN, P. 2003. On adventure therapy and the natural worlds: Respecting nature's healing. *Journal of Adventure Education and Outdoor Learning*, 3, 29–39.

BIXLER, R.D., FLOYD, M.F. & HAMMITT, W.E. 2002. Environmental socialisation: Quantitative tests of the childhood play hypothesis. *Environment and Behaviour*, 34, 795–818.

BLISS, J., ASKEW, M. & MACRAE, S. 1996. Effective teaching and learning: Scaffolding revisited. *Oxford Review of Education*, 22(1), 37–61.

BROOKES, A. 2003. A critique of neo-hahnian outdoor education theory. Part 1; Challenges to the concept of 'character building'. *Journal of Adventure Education and Outdoor Learning*, 3(1), 49–62.

BRONFENBRENNER, I.U. & MORRIS, P.A. 1998. The ecology of developmental processes. In W. DAMON & R.M. LERNER (eds), *Handbook of Child Psychology*, Vol. 1: *Theoretical Models of Human Development* (5th edn, pp. 993–1023). New York: John Wiley & Sons.

BRUCE, T. (ed.) 2012. *Early Childhood Practice: Froebel Today*. London: Sage.

BRUNER, J. 1960. *The Process of Education*. Cambridge, MA: Harvard University Press.

BUCK, T. 2011. *International Child Law* (2nd edn). Abingdon: Taylor & Francis.

CAPUTO, J.D. 1987. *Radical Hermeneutics: Repetition, Deconstruction, and the Hermeneutic Project*. Bloomington, IN: University of Indiana Press.

CARR, M. 2001. *Assessment in Early Childhood Settings*. London: Paul Chapman.

CATLING, S. 2005. Seeking younger children's 'voices' in geographical education research. *International Research in Geographical and Environmental Education*, 14, 297–304.

CERVINKA, R., RÖDERER, K. & HEFLER, E. 2012. Are nature lovers happy? On various indicators of well-being and connectedness with nature. *Journal of Health Psychology*, 17, 379–388.

CHAWLA, L. 1998. Significant life experiences revisited: A review of research on sources of environmental sensitivity. *Journal of Environmental Education*, 29, 11–21.

CHURCHILL, W. 1943. House of Commons Speech. London.

COBB, E. 1977. *The Ecology of Imagination in Childhood*. New York: Columbia University Press.

COCHRAN, K.F., DERUITER, J.A. & KING, R.A. (1993) Teacher pedagogical constructions: A recognition of pedagogical content knowledge. *Journal of Teacher Education* 44(4), 263–271.

COHEN-EMERIQUE, M. 1999. Le choc culturel. *Revue Antipodes*, 145, 11–12.

CORNELIUS, L. & HERRENKOHL, L. 2004. Power in the classroom: How the classroom environment shapes students' relationships with each other and with concepts. *Cognition and Instruction*, 22, 467–498.

COVEY, S. 1989. *7 Habits of Highly Effective People*. New York: Free Press.

DE LISI, R. 2002. From marbles to instant messenger: Implications of Piaget's ideas about peer learning. *Theory Into Practice*, 41, 5–12.

DeVRIES, R. 2000. Vygotsky, Piaget, and education: A reciprocal assimilation of theories and educational practices. *New Ideas in Psychology*, 18, 187–213.

DEWEY, J. 1997. *Experience and Education*. New York: Simon & Schuster.

DILLON, J. & WALS, A. 2008. On the danger of blurring methods, methodologies and ideologies in environmental education research. In A. REID & W. SCOTT (eds), *Researching Education and the Environment: Retrospect and Prospect* (pp. 303–312). London: Routledge.

EASEN, P.R. 1992. *Practice Development in the Primary School*. Newcastle-upon-Tyne: University of Newcastle-upon-Tyne.

EDUCATION SCOTLAND. 2012. *Making the Difference: The Impact of Staff Qualifications on Children's Learning in Early Years*. Edinburgh: Education Scotland.

EISNER, E. 1982. *Cognition and Curriculum: A Basis for Deciding What to Teach*. New York: Longman.

EISNER, E. 1991. Forms of understanding and the future of education. *Educational Researcher*, 22, 5–11.

ERIKSON, ERIK H. 1959. *Identity and the Life Cycle*. New York: International Universities Press.

ERIKSON, E. 1998. *The Life Cycle Completed: A Review*. New York and London: W.W. Norton & Company.

ERNST, J. & MONROE, M. 2004. The effects of environment-based education on students' critical thinking skills and disposition toward critical thinking. *Environmental Education Research*, 10, 507–522.

EURYDICE. 2011. *The Structure of the European Education Systems 2011/12*. Brussels: Eurydice, European Commission.

EVANS, J. & PELLEGRINI, A.D. 1997. Surplus Energy Theory: An enduring but inadequate justification for school breaktime. *Educational Review*, 49, 229.

FAIRFIELD, P. 2009. *Education after Dewey*. London: Bloomsbury.

FANG, Z. 1996. A review of research on teacher beliefs and practices. *Educational Research*, 38, 47–65.

FJORTOFT, I. & SAGEIE, J. 2000. The natural environment as a playground for children: Landscape description and analysis of a natural landscape. *Landscape and Urban Planning*, 48(1/2), 83–97.

GILL, T. 2007. *No Fear*. London: Calouste Gulbenkian Foundation.

GRAHN, J.A. MARTENSSON, F., LLINDBLAD, B., NILSON, P. & EKMAN, A. 1997. UTE pa DAGIS, Stad & Land nr. 93/1991. Alnarp: Sveriges lantbruksuniversitet.

GRUENEWALD, D.A. 2003a. The best of both worlds: A critical pedagogy of place. *Educational Researcher*, 32, 4, 3–12.

GRUENEWALD, D.A. 2003b. Foundations of place: A multidisciplinary framework for place-conscious education. *American Educational Research Journal*, 40, 619–654.

HAGEKULL, B. & HAMMARBERG, A. 2004. The role of teachers' perceived control and children's characteristics in interactions between 6-year-olds and their teachers. *Scandinavian Journal of Psychology*, 45, 301–312.

HAMMARBERG, A. & HAGEKULL, B. 2006. Changes in externalizing and internalizing behaviours over a school-year: Differences between 6-year-old boys and girls. *Infant and Child Development*, 15, 123–137.

HART, P. 2008. Requisite variety: The problem with generic guidelines for diverse genres of inquiry. In A. REID & W. SCOTT (eds), *Researching Education and the Environment: Retrospect and Prospect* (pp. 293–302). London: Routledge.

HART, R. 1992. Childrens participation: from tokenism to citizenship. Florence; UNICEF International Child Development Centre 1992, 44p. Illus. Bibliography; p44, (innocentiessays).

HEIDEGGER, M. 1927. *Being and Time*. Albany, NY: State University of New York.

HOWE, C. 1997. *Gender and Classroom Interaction: A Research Review*. [Edinburgh]: Scottish Council for Research in Education (SCRE) publication 138. Using research series 19.

HUMBERSTONE, B. 2009. 'In Splendid Isolation': Is the field missing something? Research in Outdoor Sports and Outdoor Education: Principles into practice. In I. TURCOVA & A.J. MARTIN (eds), *Outdoor Activities in Educational and Recreational Programmes*. Prague: Charles University.

INGOLD, T. 1995. Building, dwelling, living: How animals and people make themselves at home in the world. In M. STRATHERN (ed.), *Shifting Contexts: Transformations in Anthropological Knowledge*. London: Routledge.

INGOLD, T. 2000. To journey along a way of life: Maps, wayfinding and navigation. In T. INGOLD. *The Perception of the Environment: Essays in Livelihood, Dwelling and Skills* (pp. 219–242). London: Routledge.

INGOLD, T. 2006. Up, across and along. *Place and Location: Studies in Environmental Aesthetics and Semiotic*, 5, 21–36.

ISAACS, S. 1971 edition. *The Nursery Years: The Mind of the Child from Birth to Six Years*. London: Routledge.

JORDAN, M. & MARSHALL, H. 2010. Taking counselling and psychotherapy outside: Destruction or enrichment of the therapeutic frame? *European Journal of Psychotherapy & Counselling*, 12, 345–359.

KAHN JR, P.H. 1999. *The Human Relationship with Nature: Development and Culture*. Cambridge, MA: MIT Press.

KAHN JR, P.H., et al. 2010. A nature language: An agenda to catalog, save, and recover patterns of human–nature interaction. *Ecopsychology*, 2, 59–66.

KALS, E., SCHUMACHER, D. & MONTADA, L. 1999. Emotional affinity toward nature as a motivational basis to protect nature. *Environment and Behavior*, 31, 178–202.

KOLB, D.A. 1984. *Experiential Learning: Experience as the Source of Learning and Development*. Englewood Cliffs, NJ, and London: Prentice-Hall.

KOZULIN, A. 2003. Psychological tools and mediated learning. In A. KOZULIN, B. GINDIS, V.S. AGEYEV & S.M. MILLER (eds), *Vygotsky's Educational Theory in Cultural Context* (pp. 15–38). Cambridge and New York: Cambridge University Press.

KUTNIK, P., et al. 2007. The role and practice of interpersonal relationships in European early education settings: Sites for enhancing social inclusion, personal growth and learning? *European Early Childhood Education Research Journal*, 15, 379–406.

LAEVERS, F. 1997. *A Process-Oriented Child Follow-Up System for Young Children*. Leuven: Centre for Experiential Education.

LEWIS, I. 2000. Nature and adventure, *ECOS*, 1, 14–19.

LEWIS, R. 2005. *Finland, Cultural Lone Wolf.* Yarmouth, ME: Intercultural Press.

LITTLE, H. & EAGER, D. 2010. Risk, challenge and safety: Implications for play quality and playground design. *European Early Childhood Education Research Journal*, 18, 497–513.

LITTLE, H., WYVER, S. & GIBSON, F. 2011. The influence of play context and adult attitudes on young children's physical risk taking during outdoor play. *European Early Childhood Education Research Journal*, 19, 113–131.

LOTTER, C., HARWOOD, W.S. & BONNER, J.J. 2007. The influence of core teaching conceptions on teachers' use of inquiry teaching practices. *Journal of Research in Science Teaching*, 44, 1318–1347.

LOUV, R. 2005. *Last Child in the Woods: Saving our Children from Nature-Deficit Disorder.* Chapel Hill, NC: Algonquin Books of Chapel Hill.

LOUV, R. 2013. Keynote Speech in San Diego at Children & Nature Conference. San Diego, CA.

LTS (LEARNING AND TEACHING SCOTLAND) & SUSTAINABLE DEVELOPMENT EDUCATION LIAISON GROUP. 2008. *Schools Sustainable Development Education Policies: A Guide to their Preparation.* Edinburgh: LTS and Sustainable Development Education Liaison Group.

MACQUARRIE, S. 2012. *Enhancing Outdoor Learning: Strategies to Support Reflective Practice, Knowledge Transfer Project Report 2011–2013.* Auchterarder: Mindstretchers.

MACQUARRIE, S., HOWE, C. & BOYLE, J. 2012. Exploring the characteristics of small groups within science and English secondary classrooms. *Cambridge Journal of Education*, 42, 527–546.

MANNION, G., FENWICK, A., NUGENT, C. & L'ANSON, J. 2011. *Teaching in Nature.* Commissioned by Scottish Natural Heritage No. 476. Edinburgh: Scottish National Heritage.

MARTIN, P. 2004. Outdoor Education for Human/Nature Relationships. *Connections and Disconnections: Examining the Reality and Rhetoric. International Perspectives on Outdoor Education Theory and Practice.* Bendigo, Australia: La Trobe University.

MARTIN, P. 2007. Caring for the environment: Challenges from notions of caring. *Australian Journal of Environmental Education*, 23, 57–64.

MARTIN, P. 2008a. Outdoor education in senior schooling: Clarifying the body of knowledge. *Australian Journal of Outdoor Education*, 12, 13–23.

MARTIN, P. 2008b. Teacher qualification guidelines, ecological literacy and outdoor education. *Australian Journal of Outdoor Education*, 12, 32–38.

MAYNARD, T., WATERS, J. & CLEMENT, J. 2011. Moving outdoors: Further explorations of 'child-initiated' learning in the outdoor environment. *Education 3–13*, 41(3), 1–18.

MERCER, N. 2007. *Interactive Whiteboards as Pedagogic Tools in Primary Schools: Full Research Report. ESRC End of Award Report, RES-000-22-1269.* Swindon: ESRC.

MERCER, N. & LITTLETON, K. 2007. How does interaction help? In N. MERCER & K. LITTLETON. *Dialogue and the Development of Children's Thinking* (pp. 7–21). London and New York: Routledge.

MEYERS, R.B. 2008. Environmenal learning: Reflections on practice, research and theory. In A. REID & W. SCOTT (eds), *Researching Education and the Environment: Retrospect and Prospect* (pp. 213–223). London: Routledge.

MOFFETT, P.V. 2011. Outdoor mathematics trails: An evaluation of one training partnership. *Education 3–13*, 39, 277–287.

MOON, J. 1999. *Reflection in Learning and Professional Development.* London: Kogan Page.

MOORE, R.C. 1986. *Children's Domain: Play and Place in Child Development.* London: Croom Helm.

MOORE, R.C. & COSCO, N. 2000. *Developing an Earth Bound Culture through Design of Childhood Habitats*. Department of Landscape Architecture North Carolina State University.

MOORE, R.C. & WONG, H.H. 1997. *Natural Learning: The Life History of an Environmental School Yard*. Berkeley, CA: MIG Communications.

MORGAN, V. & DUNN, S. 1988. Chameleons in the classroom: Visible and invisible children in nursery and infant classrooms. *Educational Review*, 40, 3–12.

MUGNY, G. & DOISE, W. 1978. Socio-cognitive conflict and structure of individual and collective performances. *European Journal of Social Psychology*, 8, 181–192.

MULHALL, P. & GUNSTONE, R. 2008. Views about Physics held by Physics teachers with differing approaches to teaching Physics. *Research in Science Education*, 38, 435–462.

MUÑOZ, S. 2009. *Children in the Outdoors: A Literature Review*. Forres: Sustainable Development Research Centre.

NAKAMURA, J. and CSIKSZENTMIHALYI, M. 2002. The concept of flow. In C.R. SNYDER and S.J. LOPEZ (eds), *Handbook of Positive Psychology* (pp. 89–105). Oxford: Oxford University Press.

NAKAMURA, J. and CSIKSZENTMIHALYI, M. 2009. Flow theory and research. In C.R. SNYDER & S.J. LOPEZ (eds), *Oxford Handbook of Positive Psychology* (2nd edn, pp. 195–206). Oxford: Oxford University Press.

NAR (National Assessment Resource). 2013. www.educationscotland.co.uk, National assessment resource search, Auchlone Nature Kindergarten.

NESPOR, J. 1987. The role of beliefs in the practice of teaching. *Journal of Curriculum Studies*, 19, 317–328.

NICHOLS, G. 2000. Risk and adventure education. *Journal of Risk Research*, 3(2), 121–34.

NICHOLSON, S. 1971. How not to cheat the children: The theory of loose parts. *Landscape Architecture*, 62, 30–35.

NICOL, R. 2002. Outdoor environmental education in the United Kingdom: A conceptual framework of epistemological diversity and its educational implications. *Canadian Journal of Environmental Education*, 7(2), 207–23.

NICOLSON, S. 1977. How not to cheat the children: The theory of loose parts. *Landscape Architecture Quarterly*, 62(1), 30–4.

NUGENT, C. 2012. *Nature's Kindergarten: A Comparative Study*. Scottish Educational Research Conference, Ayr, Scotland.

NUNDY, S., DILLON, J. & DOWD, P. 2009. Improving and encouraging teacher confidence in out-of-classroom learning: The impact of the Hampshire Trailblazer project on 3–13 curriculum practitioners. *Education 3–13*, 37, 61–73.

NUTBROWN, C. 2012. *Foundations for Quality: Final Report of the Independent Review of Early Education and Childcare Qualifications*. London: Department for Education.

O'BRIEN, L. 2009. Learning outdoors: The forest school approach. *Education 3–13*, 37(1), 45–60.

PALINCSAR, A.S. & HERRENKOHL, L.R. 2002. Designing collaborative learning contexts. *Theory into Practice*, 41, 26–32.

PASSY, R. 2012. School gardens: Teaching and learning outside the front door. *Education* (J), 3–13, 1–16.

PELLEGRINI, A.D. 2010. Play and games mean different things in an educational context. *Nature*, 467, 27.

PYLE, R.M. 2002. Eden in a vacant lot: Special places, species and kids in the neighbourhood of life. In P. KAHN & S.R. KELLERT (eds), *Children and Nature* (pp. 305–328). Cambridge, MA: MIT Press.

QUAY, J. 2003. Experience and participation: Relating theories of learning. *Journal of Experiential Education*, 26, 105–112.

RICKINSON, M., DILLON, J., TEAMEY, K., MORRIS, M., YOUNG MEE, C., SANDERS, D. & BENEFIELD, P. 2004. *A Review of Research on Outdoor Learning*. National Foundation for Educational Research (NFER), King's College London.

ROGERS, C.R. and FREIBERG, H.J. 1994. *Freedom to Learn* (3rd edn). New York: Maxwell Macmillan.

ROGOFF, B. 1990. *Apprenticeship in Thinking: Cognitive Development in Social Context*. Oxford: Oxford University Press.

SANDSETER, E.B.H. 2007. Categorising risky play: How can we identify risk-taking in children's play? *European Early Childhood Education Research Journal*, 15, 237–252.

SANDSETER, E.B.H. 2009. Characteristics of risky play. *Journal of Adventure Education & Outdoor Learning*, 9, 3–21.

SANDSETER, E.B.H. 2010. 'It tickles in my tummy!': understanding children's risk-taking in play through reversal theory. *Journal of Early Childhood Research*, 8(1), 67–88.

SEBBA, R. 1991. The landscapes of childhood: The reflection of childhood's environment in adult memories and in children's attitudes. *Environment and Behavior*, 23, 395–422.

SHULMAN, L.S. 1986. Those who understand: Knowledge growth in teaching. *Educational Researcher*, 15(2), 4–14.

SMITH, F., HARDMAN, F. & HIGGINS, S. 2006. The impact of interactive whiteboards on teacher–pupil interaction in the National Literacy and Numeracy Strategies. *British Educational Research Journal*, 32, 443–457.

SOBEL, D. 2004. *Place-Based Education: Connecting Classrooms and Communities*. Great Barrington, MA: Orion Society.

SOBEL, D. 2008. *Childhood and Nature: Design Principles for Educators*. Portland, ME: Stenhouse Publishers.

TAYLOR, A.F., KUO, F.E. & SULLIVAN, W.C. 2001. Coping with ADD: The surprising connection to Green Play Settings. *Environment and Behaviour*, 33(1), 54–77.

TAYLOR, A.F., WILEY, A., KUO, F.E. & SULLIVAN, W.C. 1998. Growing up in the inner city: Green spaces as places to grow. *Environment & Behaviour*, 30(1), 3–27.

TURK, D.J., VAN BUSSEL, K., WAITER, G.D. & MACRAE, C.N. 2011. Mine and me: Exploring the neural basis of object ownership. *Journal of Cognitive Neuroscience*, 23, 3657–3668.

VAN DEN BOS, M., CUNNINGHAM, S.J., CONWAY, M.A. & TURK, D.J. 2010. Mine to remember: The impact of ownership on recollective experience. *Quarterly Journal of Experimental Psychology (Colchester)*, 63, 1065–1071.

VAN MANEN, M. 1990. *Researching Lived Experience: Human Science for an Action Sensitive Pedagogy*. Albany, NY, and London: State University of New York Press.

VYGOTSKY, L.S. 1962. *Thought and Language*. Cambridge, MA: MIT Press. (Original work published in 1934).

WAITE, S. 2007. 'Memories are made of this': Some reflections on outdoor learning and recall. *Education 3–13*, 35, 333–347.

WALLER, T., SANDSETER, E.B.H., WYVER, S., ARLEMALM-HAGSER, E. & MAYNARD, T. 2010. The dynamics of early childhood spaces: Opportunities for outdoor play? *European Early Childhood Education Research Journal*, 18, 437–443.

WARDEN, C. 2006. *Talking and Thinking Floorbooks*™. Auchterarder, Scotland: Mindstretchers.

WARDEN, C. 2007. *Nurture through Nature*. Working with children under three. Crieff: Mindstretchers.

WARDEN, C. 2010a. *Nature Kindergartens*. Auchterarder, Scotland: Mindstretchers.

WARDEN, C. 2010b. Creative Centre Improvement Plans – The use of graphics. Download article at: www.claire-warden.com/continuum books made by www.mindstretchers.co.uk.

WARDEN, C. 2011. Offering rich experiences. IN J. WHITE (ed.), *Outdoor Provision in the Early Years* (pp. 68–75). London: Sage.

WARDEN, C. 2012a. *Fascination of Earth: Wood Whittling*. Auchterarder, Scotland: Mindstretchers.

WARDEN, C. 2012b. *Nature Kindergartens and Forest Schools: An Exploration of Naturalistic Learning within Nature Kindergartens and Forest Schools*. Auchterarder, Scotland: Mindstretchers.

WARDEN, C. 2013a. *Facination of Air: Wind*. Crieff: Mindstretchers.

WARDEN, C. 2013b. *Fascination of Earth: Whittling*. Crieff: Mindstretchers.

WARDEN, C. 2013c. *Fascination of Fire: Charcoal*. Crieff: Mindstretchers.

WARDEN, C. 2013d. *Fascination of Water: Puddles*. Crieff: Mindstretchers.

WELLS, N.M. & EVANS, G.W. 2003. Nearby nature: A buffer of life stress among Rural Children. *Environment & Behaviour*, 35(3), 311–330.

WENGER, E. 1999. *Communities of Practice: Learning, Meaning, and Identity*. Cambridge: Cambridge University Press.

WHITEHEAD, J. & McNIFF, J. 2006. *Action Research: Living Theory*. London: Sage.

WILSON, E.O. 1984. *Biophilia*. Cambridge, MA: Harvard University Press.

WOOD, D. & WOOD, H. 1996. Vygotsky, tutoring and learning. *Oxford Review of Education*, 22, 5–16.

WYVER, S., LITTLE, H., TRANTER, P., BUNDY, A., NAUGHTON, G. & SANDSETER, E.B.H. 2010. Ten ways to restrict children's freedom to play: The problem of surplus safety. *Contemporary Issues in Early Childhood*, 11, 263–277.

Index